NEFYN, MORFA NEFYN
and PORTH DINLLAEN

NEFYN, MORFA NEFYN and PORTH DINLLAEN

Personalities, Events and Incidents
1880 – Present

Roland Bond

First published in 2012

© Roland Bond / Gwasg Carreg Gwalch

Copyright © by Llygad Gwalch 2011.
All rights reserved. No part of this publication
may be reproduced or transmitted, in any form
or by any means, without permission.

ISBN: 978-184524-190-2

Published by
Llygad Gwalch,
12 Iard yr Orsaf, Llanrwst, Wales LL26 0EH
tel: 01492 642031
fax: 01492 641502
e-mail: books@carreg-gwalch.com
www.carreg-gwalch.com

This book is dedicated to the memory of two fine Welsh gentlemen – my late father-in-law, Hugh Lloyd Roberts; and the late Richard John Hughes of Nefyn who taught me so much about the history of the parish and its people.

Acknowledgements

As always, I am grateful to the members of staff at the Gwynedd Archives, Caernarfon, for their invaluable help in assisting me to locate appropriate archive material. I also wish to express my thanks to Dr Robyn Léwis who prompted me to write this second volume and whose suggestions have been greatly appreciated. I am also indebted to Mrs Mair Spencer, Mrs Len Williams and Mr Eirwyn Jones for the photographs and the information which they have so willingly supplied. I am extremely grateful to Miss Clare Smith for her colour photographs of Nefyn and the surrounding area, and to Miss Swyn Spencer for the photographs which she took in Patagonia. Finally, I would like to thank my wife, Enfys, for her constant help and support during the preparation of this book, and my son, Jonathan for his technical assistance.

Contents

Preface — 10

1. The Closing Decades of the Nineteenth Century 1880-1899 — 11
Introduction — 11
The *SS Cyprian* and the RNLI Board of Inquiry 1881 — 15
Three Important Shipowning Brothers-in-law from Nefyn — 17
Nefyn Loses its Borough Status 1882 — 20
The Nefyn Town Trust — 21
Further attempts to turn Porth Dinllaen into an important port — 21
Undersea Cables Between Abergeirch and Ireland — 22
Lloyd George, the Nefyn Fishermen and the By-Election of 1890 — 23
The First Nefyn Show 1891 — 25
An 'Invasion' of Nefyn — 26
The Building of the Madryn Hall 1898 — 27
Nefyn Football Club, late 19th Century – Present — 28

2. The Early 20th Century 1900-1914 — 31
Introduction — 31
Lloyd George, the People of Nefyn and the Boer War — 34
Two More Attempts to Bring the Railway to Nefyn and Porth Dinllaen — 35
A Nefyn Sailor's Bravery during a Foreign Earthquake, 1905 — 36
The Building of a Reservoir for Nefyn 1906 — 36
The Founding of Nefyn Golf Club 1907 — 37
The Opening of Morfa Nefyn School 1908 — 38
An Unusual Lifeboat Accident at Porth Dinllaen 1913 — 39
A Fatal Accident at the Gwylwyr Quarry 1914 — 40

3. The Great War 1914-1918 — 41
Introduction — 41
The Early Days of the War — 43
The People at Home in Nefyn — 44
Conscription 1916 — 45
The Revd J. Ellis Williams at the National Eisteddfod 1916 — 46
The Sinking of *HMS Hampshire* 1916 — 46
Three Fatal Wartime Accidents in Nefyn — 48
The Sinking of the *SS Dora*, 1917 — 49
Bodies Washed up on the Northern Coast of Llŷn 1918 — 50
War-time Visitors to Nefyn — 51

The Death of Sergeant McCurdy 1918	51
The Cessation of Hostilities 1918	52
The Influenza Pandemic of 1918-19	52
Nefyn and Morfa Nefyn Sailors during the Great War	53
Nefyn and Morfa Nefyn Soldiers during the Great War	56

4. The Inter-War Years 1919-1939 — 60

Introduction	60
The *North Anglia* Tragedy 1922	64
The Nefyn and Morfa Nefyn War Memorials 1923	73
Jane Jones, Tŷ Coch Inn, Porth Dinllaen	74
The Final Attempt to Extend the Railway to Nefyn 1924	75
The Revd John Owen Williams at Nefyn	76
Nefyn Fishermen and the Marauding Seals 1925	77
The Solar Eclipse of 1927	78
A Ship Beached at Porth Dinllaen 1927	78
A Nefyn Sea Captain's Gallantry Award 1929	79
The Porth Dinllaen Coastguard Station Established about 1930	80
The Revd Tom Nefyn Williams	81
The Rescue of Two Sea Planes at Porth Dinllaen 1933	83
John Glyn Davies	83
A Nefyn Night Watchman and the Great Fire of 1936	84
Urdd Gobaith Cymru at Porth Dinllaen	87
Elizabeth Watkin-Jones, the Children's Author	88
Henry Parry of Montclare	89
The Gough Family of Gorse Cliff	90

5. The Second World 1939-1945 — 94

Introduction	94
Protection against Invasion in the Nefyn Area	98
The Nefyn Home Guard	98
Air-Raid Precautions	101
The Royal Observer Corps	102
RAF Nefyn	102
Evacuees from Liverpool	104
Lord Haw Haw and Enemy Spies	107
The Prisoner of War Camp in Nefyn	108
Aircraft and Shipping Incidents in the Nefyn Area	109
The Voluntary Services and Fund Raising	111
Agriculture and Food	112
Wartime Cultural Life and Entertainment	113

The Welcome Home and Victory Celebrations	114
Local Personnel who Served in the Armed Forces during World War II	114
Nefyn and Morfa Merchant Seamen during World War II	115
Some of the Local Men were Commended during the War	118
Sub-Lieutenant Michael Wynn RNVR	120

6. The Post-Second World War Years: 1945 – Present 124

Introduction	124
Violet Millar of Caeau Capel and a British Prime Minister	129
An Heroic Beach Rescue 1948	130
The Rose Queen Festival and the Nefyn Carnival	131
The Drowning of Two Nefyn Lads 1950	132
Nefyn and the Llŷn Pilgrimage of 1950	133
The Last Great Herring Catch at Nefyn 1950	134
A Young Nefyn Man is Drowned at Bodeilias 1952	135
A Library for Nefyn 1955	135
Nefyn Sailing Club 1957	137
Professor Herbert Rees Wilson	137
The Nefyn Street-Naming Rumpus of the 1960s	140
Nefyn and the 1969 Investiture	140
R. Gerallt Jones	141
The Fire on Garn Boduan 1979	142
RNLI Medals for Porth Dinllaen Lifeboatmen	143
The Burning of a Nefyn Holiday Home 1979	144
The Opening of the Nefyn Maritime Museum 1979	144
John Ifor Davies	145
The Llŷn Earthquake of 1984	147
The Twinning of Nefyn with Porth Madryn 1998	147
A Fatal Landslide at Nefyn 2001	149
Graffiti Daubing at Nefyn 2002	151
Doctor Robyn Léwis	152
O Ddrws i Ddrws 2003	153
The Most Photographed Place in Llŷn	153
A New Primary Health Care Centre for Nefyn 2007	154
A New Inn Sign for the Bryncynan Inn 2007	154
The Sea Claims a Nefyn Fisherman 2008	156
A Special Area	157
A New Community Centre for Nefyn 2010	157
Nefyn Girl Duffy Rises to International Stardom	157

Bibliography and Sources 160

Preface

This book is the sequel to *Nefyn: The Story of an Ancient Gwynedd Town and Parish*, which dealt with many of the important themes in Nefyn's history and some of the significant changes that have occurred in the parish over the centuries. This current volume complements the first Nefyn book, for it continues the story over the past 130 years, since the previous voume scarcely ventured beyond the beginning of the 20th century.

As its title suggests, this book deals with certain personalities associated with the area during that period, and it narrates many of the notable events and occurrences that have happened since 1880. The period from the closing years of the 19th century to the present day has been one of tremendous change and upheaval, including two world wars. Consequently the Nefyn of today is a very different place from that of the late Victorian era.

It is important to mention that a totally different approach has been employed in the writing of this book. Unlike the first book, which embodied a thematic approach, the story since 1880 is divided chronologically into six chapters, each one covering a clearly-defined part of the entire period. For example, the story begins in Chapter 1 with 'The Closing Decades of the 19th Century: 1880-1899' and it ends in Chapter 6 with 'The Post-Second World War Years: 1945 – Present Day'.

Each of the six chapters commences with an introductory piece of text which sets out a general overview of the period covered, and which relates local matters to important events and trends nationally. Then each chapter goes on to deal with certain noteworthy personalities associated with Nefyn, as well as significant happenings and events that have occurred within the parish during those years. For example, Chapter 1 (1880-99) opens with an account of the catastrophic wreck of the SS Cyprian in 1881 and the subsequent locally-held RNLI Board of Inquiry; the final chapter (1945-Present) concludes with an account of the rise to international fame during 2008-9 of Nefyn-born soul singer-songwriter, Duffy. Thus the story is brought right up to date.

Chapter 1

The Closing Decades of the Nineteenth Century 1880-1899

Introduction
As already suggested in the preface, in the 1880s and 1890s Nefyn and the surrounding district was a very different place from that of today, for 130 years ago the population was engaged principally in agriculture, fishing, quarrying and maritime activity.

In 1881 the parish contained 44 farms of varying sizes, and farming was still highly labour intensive. Consequently many people earned a living as farmers, agricultural labourers or domestic farm servants. Granite quarrying was still prospering, and the Nefyn quarries at Gwylwyr, Bodeilias and Foel Dywyrch continued to provide employment for many local men and boys. The brickworks at Bwlch, Morfa Nefyn, were still in production.

A considerable number of Nefyn men were fishermen, for there was still a large fleet of small fishing boats working from Porth Nefyn. Porth Dinllaen remained an important little port which served the villages and farmsteads of the northern part of Llŷn. As late as 1880, 128 ships brought essential supplies inwards during the year, while 84 vessels carried goods out, mainly agricultural produce.

Huge numbers of men from the parish served as sea captains and sailors, manning locally-owned sailing vessels based in local ports such as Caernarfon, Porthmadog and Pwllheli, as well as ships belonging to the large Welsh-owned, Liverpool-based shipping companies. According to the *Mercantile Navy List* of 1881, there were still 57 sailing vessels owned and managed at Nefyn. They were mostly wooden-built schooners and brigs, although the list also included some large barques and fully-rigged ships, managed by important and influential shipowners like John Thomas (Iorwerth) John Baugh Jarrett (Fron Oleu) William Thomas (Bodlondeb) Robert Rees, (Penllel), John Roberts (Tanybryn, Morfa), Owen Griffith (Plas) and the North Wales Shipping Company.

Men from Nefyn not only sailed the coasts of Britain but they also traversed the oceans of the world on three-masted schooners and barques. Local people who could afford to do so, as well as other folk throughout North Wales, invested their savings in local shipping enterprises like the Nefyn-based North Wales Shipping Company. At the start of this period ship insurance was also booming in Nefyn, where the local insurance societies covered not only locally-owned ships but also vessels based in some of the larger ports like Liverpool, Cardiff, Newcastle and London.

But these two decades were witnessing huge changes in the maritime world. There were signs that the days of the wooden sailing vessel were numbered. The building of wooden ships on local beaches had already ceased. The last vessel to be built at Porth Dinllaen was the *Annie Lloyd* which was completed in 1876, while the *Venus* was the last ship to leave the stocks at Porth Nefyn in 1880. As the railways expanded and as the roads improved, the coastal shipping trade declined both locally and nationally, and therefore more and more Nefyn men were manning the larger ocean-going vessels. Furthermore, many ship owners and local sailors had begun to show a preference for iron-built sailing ships and steamships. The purchase of the iron barques, *Eivion* and *Gwynedd*, by the North Wales Shipping Company, and the establishment of the Prydain Steamship Company at Nefyn, were signs of the changing times.

During the late 19th century the Nefyn ship insurance societies, which had focused mainly upon wooden sailing vessels, began to decline. By 1885 only 303 vessels were insured at Nefyn, and by 1890 the Nefyn societies had ceased to exist altogether, apart from the 'Provincial Society' and the 'Carnarvon and Nevin Association', both of which lasted until 1901.

The rocky northern coastline of Llŷn remained a danger to shipping in stormy weather, and the Porth Dinllaen lifeboat was frequently called upon to assist sailing vessels and steamships in distress. Despite the presence of the Porth Dinllaen lifeboat and the Morfa Nefyn life-saving team, mariners continued to lose their lives along this coast, as in the case of the *SS Cyprian* which was wrecked near Porth Dinllaen in 1881. In October 1888 a new lifeboat arrived at the station. Like her immediate predecessor she was a 12-oared boat named the *George Moore*, but she was two feet longer than the previous vessel. Therefore a new boathouse and slipway had to be constructed at a cost of £1414-12s-0d.

Before the end of the 19th century further plans were drawn up to bring the railway to Porth Dinllaen in order to establish it as a viable steamer port operating in direct competition with Holyhead, but those plans came to nothing.

By modern-day standards, life in Nefyn was primitive. The roads remained unsurfaced, and most people moved around the parish on foot. Locally-owned horse-drawn coaches were operating regular services between Nefyn, Morfa Nefyn, Edern and Pwllheli, although some people travelled beyond the parish boundary on horseback or by pony and trap.

Goods were transported around the peninsula by horse-drawn wagon or by donkey and cart. The local water supply was Ffynnon Fair (*Saint Mary's well*) at the top of Stryd y Ffynnon, and the task of carrying water was a daily chore for every household in the parish. Ordnance Survey maps of the period show that outlying areas, like Mynydd Nefyn and Morfa village, had their own supplies of water in the form of springs and wells. Cottages and houses were heated by coal fires, and regular supplies of coal were delivered to the beaches at Nefyn and Porth Dinllaen by small steam-powered coasters. Lighting was provided by oil lamps and candles.

There was a bank in Nefyn – Pugh Jones & Company (Stryd Fawr) which later became the Metropolitan Bank of England and Wales. There had been a Post Office in the town since 1843, and by this time it had been granted money order, savings bank and telegraph office status. However, it was still under the jurisdiction of the Pwllheli Post Office, via which all mail was delivered. There were also two local insurance societies, Clwb Mawr in Y Maes and the Oddfellows Society (known as Madryn Lodge) in Stryd y Llan. There was both a Conservative Club (Tower Terrace) and a Liberal Club (Town Hall).

Nefyn and Morfa Nefyn were almost self-sufficient in meeting the daily needs of their inhabitants. Directories of the period inform us that, within the parish, there were bakers, butchers, confectioners, grocers and tea merchants, flour dealers, boot and shoe makers, drapers, dress makers and tailors, milliners and hatters, watchmakers, lamp and oil merchants, ironmongers, blacksmiths, stationers and newsagents, building contractors, solicitors and a surgeon. In addition, Nefyn possessed two hotels (the Nanhoron Arms and the Sportsman), nine lodging houses and four taverns (the Bull at the lower end of the town, the Madryn Arms in Stryd Fawr and the Prince of Wales and the White Horse in Stryd Moreia). The Newborough Arms in Stryd y Ffynnon closed in the early 1880s. In 1889-90 Nefyn fairs were still being held three times a year.[1]

By the 1880s Nefyn was attracting some relatively wealthy English visitors during the summer season. A few of the most affluent families would arrive in their own carriages for the entire summer, hiring local houses which had stabling for the horse and an outhouse for the carriage. Others would arrive as fare-paying passengers on the horse-drawn coach from Pwllheli railway station, and they would stay for one or two weeks at one of the inns, lodging houses or apartments in the town. An 1886 Directory[2] states that the town 'is much frequented by visitors during the summer.' It refers to the fine sandy beach, the exceptionally safe bathing, the pure bracing air and the magnificent scenery. It mentions 'the good old-fashioned hostelry, the Nanhoron Arms, with its excellent accommodation and moderate tariff' as well as many 'excellent lodging houses.' There are also several advertisements for private holiday apartments, as well as one or two fully-furnished houses for hire. Writing about Nefyn in August 1893, the *Caernarfon and Denbigh Herald* stated, 'All at once a large influx of visitors took place here last Saturday. The town is now full. It is to be regretted that more lodging houses are not built here.'[3]

The majority of the children in the parish attended the Nefyn Board School, which was an all age school where the pupils remained until they attained the age of 13. Those children from Morfa Nefyn who lived at the Edern end of the village would have attended the Edern School. At 13 years of age children entered the world of work, the majority of the boys embarking upon a career at sea, on a farm or in one of the quarries, while most girls entered service as domestic servants. There were two private schools at Morfa Nefyn and Porth Dinllaen. In the 1880s Mrs Hugh Jones's 'Ladies Select School' at Plas Tirion catered for boarders as well as day pupils, who were given 'instruction in English, French, German, Music, Singing, Drawing and all kinds of Plain and Fancy Needlework', while for many years Mrs Jane Jones ran a private school for the children of mariners at the Tŷ Coch Inn, Porth Dinllaen.

Most people attended religious worship every Sunday, and they were overwhelmingly Nonconformist. There were four flourishing Nonconformist chapels in Nefyn, three of which had to be rebuilt in order to accommodate their growing congregations – the large Calvinistic Methodist Capel Isa in Stryd y Ffynnon (rebuilt 1875), the Independent Capel Soar at Penybryn (rebuilt 1880) and the Wesleyan Methodist Chapel in Stryd Moreia (rebuilt 1881). There was also the Baptist chapel on Y Fron. In addition, there was the Calvinistic Methodist Capel Pisgah on Mynydd Nefyn and three chapels in Morfa Nefyn – Caersalem (Baptist), Moriah (Methodist) and Tabernacl (Independent).

The Nonconformist chapels, which were noted for their inter-denominational rivalry, remained at the heart of Welsh-language culture with their choirs, literary societies and eisteddfodau. The local eisteddfod became a passion in Wales during the closing years of the 19th century and in the period before the Great War. Anglican services were held in the old Saint Mary's Church, Penisa'r dre, and at the new Church of Sant Mair in Morfa Nefyn, which had been built in 1871.

The Established Church, which was supported by the anglicised landed gentry, was viewed with great suspicion by most Welsh Nonconformists. They viewed it as the English Church whose bishops until very recently had not even been able to speak Welsh. Nationally, voices from within the chapels were becoming more powerful. The Welsh Sunday Closing Act of 1881 combined a sense of Welshness, with teetotalism and Sunday observance, while there were many Welsh voices clamouring for a disestablished Church in Wales.

In 1880 Nefyn possessed a population of about 1,800 people. Most of the inhabitants had been born in Nefyn or in neighbouring Llŷn parishes. The town had attracted some inward migration from England (especially quarry workers from Leicestershire) as well as a few people from other parts of north and mid Wales. Although at this time Nefyn was a bustling, buoyant community it was no longer the important place that it had been centuries earlier when the Black Prince granted the town its charter. Therefore at the start of this period the town lost its borough status.

In the industrial parts of South Wales, and in the border regions, the Welsh language was under threat from English-speakers, but in Nefyn, in the Welsh heartland, Welsh was still the language used in the home, the street and the chapel. The 1891 Census reveals that the majority of parishioners spoke only Welsh. Some inhabitants were bilingual, but they were mainly mariners who travelled a great deal, as well as people engaged in some form of business. After a time the Nefyn-born descendents of the English quarrymen who had moved to the town became Welsh speakers and they were quickly assimilated into the community as Welsh men and women.

By the end of the 19th century there were signs that the influence of the local wealthy landowners had begun to wane. Acts of Parliament which were passed during the 1880s afforded more people the right to vote. The establishment of the County Councils in 1889 eroded the power and influence of the Llŷn squirearchy even further. Traditionally the local landed gentry, like the Newborough family of Boduan and Glynllifon and the Jones Parry family of Madryn Castle, had held the most important positions of authority, and over the years a succession of such men had been returned as Members of Parliament for the Caernarfon Boroughs, including Nefyn. But things were about to change. During this period, an energetic and radical young man who came from much humbler beginnings would be elected as the Member of Parliament to represent the people of Nefyn. His name was David Lloyd George.

The *SS Cyprian* and the RNLI Board of Inquiry 1881

In October 1881 there occurred an event that is remembered for three reasons – the selflessness of one man, the heroism of several others and a subsequent local Board of Inquiry arranged by the RNLI.

On the 13th October, 1881 the 940 ton steamer *SS Cyprian*, captained by

Captain John Alexander Strachan, set out from Liverpool bound for Genoa with a mixed cargo. During the night, as she crossed Caernarfon Bay in a ferocious north-westerly gale, one of her boilers broke down. The master kept the ship going on the other boiler until, at 8.30 the following morning, the steering gear also failed. Shortly after that the fire in the second boiler was extinguished by water entering the engine room. Since the vessel was within sight of the Llŷn coast, the captain decided to drop the ship's anchors in order to ride out the storm. Unfortunately both anchor chains snapped, leaving the ship completely at the mercy of the wind and the waves.

Fearing the worst, Captain Strachan distributed the ship's lifejackets to his crew only to discover a young stowaway on board. Immediately he unfastened his own lifejacket and gave it to the boy, saying that he would swim to the shore if necessary.

A few Nefyn inhabitants, standing on top of the cliffs, had noticed the Cyprian but they believed that she was heading for Porth Dinllaen. However, the stricken vessel was forced straight on. At 5.30 pm the *Cyprian* was driven onto jagged rocks off Cwmhistir, approximately two miles southwest of Porth Dinllaen, where she started to break up very quickly.

Two local farmers, who were working in a field overlooking the sea, had seen the ship founder, and they rushed down to the shore. Other local people soon joined them. They could see that the ship was disintegrating and many of the crew members were floundering in the violent seas. Some were being swept towards the shore and hurled against the rocks while others were being dragged under the water.

The Porth Dinllaen lifeboat crew was alerted, but the coxswain, Hugh Davies, considered it too dangerous to attempt a launch in such appalling conditions. He called out the Morfa Nefyn Lifesaving Apparatus Team, but the wind was so strong that they found it impossible to fire the rockets carrying the lifelines.

Some local men bravely scrambled over the rocks from where they attempted to reach some of the crew members who were struggling desperately to reach the shore. Police Sergeant Roberts from Morfa Nefyn was almost swept away. A local quarryman, David Jones, did manage to rescue one sailor, while Richard Roberts, another local quarryman who had previously been a seaman, managed to drag seven others to safety.

Eight persons were saved that evening, including the young stowaway, and they were taken to local farms and cottages to be cared for. But the captain and seventeen members of his crew were drowned. Their bodies were later recovered and taken to the coach house at the Cefn Amwlch Arms Inn in Edern. Eventually they were interred in an unmarked mass grave in

Edern churchyard, but the captain's body was returned to Liverpool for burial.

However, that was not the end of the matter, for the incident had hit the headlines. The selfless act of Captain Strachan was later to become the subject of a sermon in Westminster Abbey. For his bravery Richard Roberts was awarded a 'Life Saving Certificate' by the Liverpool Shipwreck and Humane Society. Each of the other local people who took part in the rescue were rewarded by the Squire of Nanhoron with the gift of a certificate, a medal and a gold sovereign.

But so many questions were asked about the failure of the lifeboat to go the assistance of the *Cyprian*'s crew that the RNLI decided to hold an official Board of Inquiry. It consisted of ten of the most experienced master mariners in the area. After they had heard evidence from all available witnesses, they came to their conclusion – it would have been impossible to launch the lifeboat in such horrific conditions, and no lifeboat crew could have rowed against such hostile seas. The coxswain and crew of the Porth Dinllaen lifeboat had been exonerated!

A wealthy lady from Henley-on-Thames was so moved by the story of the *Cyprian* that she donated the sum of £800 for the purchase of a new lifeboat to serve along the Caernarfonshire coast. Appropriately named the *Cyprian*, it was later installed at the nearby Trefor station.

In 1943, over 60 years after the *SS Cyprian* had been wrecked, Nefyn Parish Council decided to place a memorial stone in Edern churchyard over the spot where the crew members of the vessel had been buried. The unveiling of that memorial stone was reported in the *Caernarfon and Denbigh Herald*, dated 7th March, 1943. To this day a few iron remnants of the *Cyprian*, including the ship's two boilers, can still be seen scattered in the small bay near Cwmistir, and one or two items from the wrecked ship are now among the artefacts in the Nefyn Maritime Museum.

Three Important Shipowning Brothers-in-law from Nefyn
Throughout the second half of the 19th century Nefyn was an important and busy maritime centre, where many sailing ships of various sizes were owned. Two Nefyn-born brothers-in-law, each with the surname 'Thomas', were pre-eminent in local shipping affairs, while a third became one of the leading Welsh shipowners in the port of Liverpool. Captain William Thomas, Bodlondeb, Captain John Thomas, Iorwerth and Robert Thomas of Cricieth and Liverpool all married daughters of Thomas Rees of Pistyll Farm.

William Thomas, who was born in 1826, married Gwen Rees, the third daughter of Thomas Rees. In 1861 he is recorded as a sail and rope maker and a farmer of 20 acres, living at Ty'n y Coed, Nefyn. By 1871 he is listed as a 'Manager of Shipping Insurance' at Nefyn for, as we have already noted, the town had become an important centre for ship insurance. It is known that he had a shipping insurance office at Number 2 Marine Terrace on the Morfa Road.

By 1881 he was living at Bodlondeb where he was recorded as 'Shipowner and Agent of Marine Insurance Society'. Two sons were also involved in the shipping business, one as a ship broker and the other as an insurance clerk. At this time William Thomas owned two barques – the 760 ton wooden vessel *Medusa*, built at Maitland, Nova Scotia, and the three-masted iron barque *Queen of Cambria* which had been built at Hylton. For many years the *Queen of Cambria* sailed to Australia, the Far East and the west coast of South America, and she made frequent sailings round the Horn. Two of her shareholders were Robert Rees Penllel, his wife's brother, and Robert Thomas, his wife's brother-in-law.

When the North Wales Shipping Company was established in Nefyn in 1875 William Thomas became its manager but, owing to a downturn in the economic climate generally and in the shipping world in particular, the company was wound up in 1887, and its two vessels, the *Evion* and the *Gwynedd*, were sold off.

William Thomas died in 1898 by which time the days of the large sailing vessel were numbered, as more and more shipowners began to purchase steam- powered vessels.

John Thomas, born in 1831, was the son of old John John Thomas of Fron Oleu, a legendary Nefyn figure during the early 19th century, who was a fisherman, shipowner, farmer, and the most important of the early Nefyn shipbuilders.

Captain John Thomas married Mary Rees, the second daughter of Pistyll Farm. By 1851 at the age of 20, he is recorded as a master mariner, living at Fron Oleu, the former home of his father who had died in 1844. Subsequently he owned and managed a large fleet of ships, and in 1881 he is listed as the owner two large Canadian-built wooden barques, the *J. P. Smith* (772 tons) and the *Wandering Sprite* (781 tons) as well as the *Christiana*.

By 1881 he was living at Iorwerth Villa where he was recorded as a 'retired master mariner and shipowner'. He was a Justice of the Peace and also a director of the Nefyn Marine Insurance Societies. He died in 1913, just prior to the outbreak of the Great War.

Robert Thomas, the third member of this trio of brothers-in-law, was born in Abererch in March 1848, but his family moved to Tai Lôn, Nefyn, when Robert was a young lad. His father was a ships' carpenter, helping to construct the sailing vessels which were being built at Porth Nefyn. In 1861 Robert Thomas was a pupil teacher at the Nefyn British School which had recently moved into its new building on the Morfa Road.

It is almost certain that many of Robert's contemporaries would have followed in the family tradition of a career at sea. Robert clearly had different ideas. Imbued with entrepreneurial ambitions, he set himself up in business as a commercial traveller dealing in drapery, and travelling as far as Liverpool to sell his wares. In 1871 at the age of 22 he was lodging at the home of a dress maker in Queens Road, Everton, probably one of his customers. In 1873 he married Elizabeth Rees, another of the Pistyll Farm daughters. Even though he was selling drapery, it is known that he had a financial interest in ships, for he invested in some of the ships operated by his brother-in-law, William Thomas, Bodlondeb.

By the early 1880s he had moved to Cricieth where he set up his own shipping company. Obviously there was more money to be made out of shipping than selling fabrics! He bought managing-owner shares in both wooden and iron barques, and he was clearly a shrewd business man, for he bought older ships at bargain prices. For example, he purchased at a 'knock-down' price both the *Gwynedd* and the *Eivion* when those two Nefyn companies were wound up. By the 1890s he was able to order five new iron vessels!

At first his registered office was Bryntiron Terrace, Cricieth, but in 1893 he moved to 49 High Street, Cricieth. By May 1899 he had left Cricieth for Liverpool where he established his registered office at Richmond Buildings, 26 Chapel Street, and where his firm's telegraphic address was 'Gwladgarwr' (patriot). In 1901 Robert Thomas and his family were living at an address in Bentley Road, Toxteth Park, Liverpool.

By 1905 the Thomas fleet consisted of 15 large sailing ships, many of them named after Welsh castles. His famous Welsh castle vessels, including '*Gwrtheyrn Castle, Criccieth Castle, Deudraeth Castle, Penrhyn Castle, Powys Castle, Conway Castle, Gwydyr Castle, Harlech Castle, Rhuddlan Castle* and *Dolbadarn Castle*' reads like part of the index to a book on North Wales castles. Almost all of his shareholders came from North Wales, and they included the schoolmaster at Nefyn Board School. David Lloyd George had an association with Robert Thomas & Company. The registration document for the *Powys Castle* was presented by Lloyd George & Company in January 1892, and Lloyd George, as well as other members of his family including his father-in-law, were among the shareholders of some of Robert Thomas's ships. Many of the captains and sailors who manned the Robert Thomas fleet came from Nefyn.

When Robert Thomas died in June 1908, a few years before the outbreak of the Great War, Robert Rees Thomas, his son, continued to manage the business. Unlike many other companies, Robert Thomas & Company kept faith with their old sailing vessels throughout the war, despite the fact that they were considered to be easy targets for German U-boats. Indeed the war years did take a heavy toll on the Robert Thomas fleet. In 1915 the *Penrhyn Castle* went missing. The *Conway Castle* was also sunk in 1915, while the *Neotsfield* and the *Belford* were both torpedoed in 1917.

Before the war had ended Robert Rees Thomas and the other directors decided to sell off their remaining ships and wind up the company. In selling up when they did, they achieved very attractive prices for their vessels, and this brought handsome rewards for the company's investors.

Therefore towards the end of the Great War, Robert Thomas & Company faded from the maritime scene along with the large, square-rigged sailing ship. Thus came to an end one of the great Welsh, Liverpool-based, shipping enterprises – a company founded by the son of a ships' carpenter, brought up in Tai Lôn, Nefyn.

Nefyn Loses its Borough Status 1882
At the time of the Welsh Princes, Nefyn had been a very important town in Llŷn and one of the leading ports and economic centres in the Kingdom of Gwynedd. Under the English Crown it continued to thrive and in 1355 it was granted borough status, the original charter having been sealed on the instructions of Edward the Black Prince from his chancery at Caernarfon.

But by the 1880s Nefyn had become a mere shadow of her former self. Over the years the population had remained fairly modest and static, and the administration of the borough had been allowed to decay. In 1833 an official inquiry had criticised the way in which its affairs were administered. Although some leading figures in the town subsequently brought about a number of improvements, it was a case of 'too little too late'. Pwllheli had superseded Nefyn as the most important urban and economic centre in Llŷn, while Porth Nefyn was no longer a port of any significance, since Porth Dinllaen had become the chief port along the northern coast of the peninsula. Consequently, under the terms of the Municipal Corporations Act of 1882, the historic borough of Nefyn was dissolved, and it reverted to a parish.

However, for many years a curious anomaly remained. Although officially Nefyn had lost its borough status, for the purposes of Parliamentary elections it remained one of the six Caernarfon Boroughs, along with Caernarfon, Bangor, Conwy, Pwllheli and Cricieth.

The Nefyn Town Trust

The Nefyn Town Trust is a registered charity which was established to look after the land and property which remained as 'permanent endowment' following the dissolution of Nefyn Corporation. The responsibilities of the Trust also included managing the income which accrued from the properties in its care.

Since the Trust was first established, several properties have been disposed of, including the Madryn Hall which was demolished in 2006. At present the Trust is responsible for the following:

- 26 houses which are leased to tenants
- 1 small house, used as a Trust office
- 6 garages, converted from old cottages
- 2 store rooms, also former cottages
- 2 areas of land

In addition the Trust is the guardian of Ffynnon Fair, the old Saint Mary's well, which is situated just below Y Groes, and the watchtower at Pen y Bryn, both of which are Grade II listed buildings. The Trust is responsible for the repair, maintenance and insurance of all the properties in its care and for any other expenditure relating to them.

When the Trust has met all its financial obligations it uses any remaining monies to support and assist other organisations for the benefit of the local community. The Nefyn Town Trust is run by a number of Trustees including a Chairman, a Secretary/Clerk and a Treasurer, and the members usually meet monthly. The Trust Office is Gwalia Bach in Stryd Moreia.

Further attempts to turn Porth Dinllaen into an important port

At one time Porth Dinllaen, with its fine natural harbour in the lee of Penrhyn Porth Dinllaen, had been a serious contender in the race to become the main embarkation port and packet station for Ireland rather than Holyhead. Following the building of Telford's suspension bridge across the Menai Strait in 1826 and Stephenson's tubular steel bridge in 1850, and after improvements had been made to the harbour at Holyhead in the middle of the 19th century, the contest was virtually over.

However, some people refused to give up the idea of Porth Dinllaen becoming an important port. In 1877 Cambrian Railways promoted an Act of Parliament for the building of an extension of the Cambrian Line to Porth Dinllaen, as well as the construction of a pier in the bay. However, owing to opposition from other railway companies, the Act never reached the statute book.

In 1884 a group of local people, including Love Jones Parry of Madryn Castle, formed a company called 'The Porthdinllaen Railway Company'. At this time Love Jones Parry was the sitting Member of Parliament for the Caernarfon Boroughs, and an Act of Parliament was passed to allow a branch line to be constructed from the Cambrian Line at Abererch to Porth Dinllaen. Although the time limit for the completion of the project was twice extended to 1888 and 1892, the £102,000 capital required for the undertaking was not forthcoming, and so the work to extend the railway to Porth Dinllaen failed to advance beyond the planning stage.

In 1897 plans for a railway line from Pwllheli to Porth Dinllaen were revived. The ambitious scheme included the building of quays and a pier in the bay, protected by a huge breakwater connected to the rocks at Carreg y Chwislen. The intention was to establish a regular steamboat service between Porth Dinllaen and Wicklow in competition with the Holyhead-Dublin crossing. This renewed interest arose because the authorities in Wicklow had already spent a considerable sum of money on strengthening their breakwater and deepening their harbour. But the work at Porth Dinllaen was never started, almost certainly owing to lack of investment.

Undersea Cables Between Abergeirch and Ireland

Just west of Porth Dinllaen is a small bay and river mouth called Abergeirch, which visitors to the area have usually referred to as 'Cable Bay'. In 1886 this inlet was chosen as the terminus for a new telegraph cable between Ireland and North Wales, and subsequently other telegraph and telephone cables from Ireland came ashore here. But the 1886 cable was not the first telegraphic link between North Wales and Ireland. As early as 1852, telegraph cables had been laid between Holyhead and Ireland, and others followed during the late 1850's and 1860's.

When the new 1886 cable was laid a small hut was built at Abergeirch to house the machinery connected to the cable, and a manually-operated telegraph relay office was established at Plas Tirion, Morfa Nefyn. In 1891, according to the census for that year, an Irishman, John Wales, was living at Plas Tirion with his family. He was the first telegraphist in charge of the station. In 1892 a second telegraph cable was laid between Abergeirch and Newcastle, County Wicklow.

In 1898 the first telephone cable was laid under the Irish Sea from Abergeirch to Newcastle, and in 1901 another Irishman, John Nevin McCurdy, was in charge of the Morfa Nefyn station. By this time the telegraph/telephone relay office had been moved to purpose-built premises across the road from Plas Tirion, and John McCurdy and his family were living at Sunnyside. When the Great War broke out McCurdy joined the army, was sent to France as a specialist telegraph/telephone operator with the rank of sergeant, but sadly, as we shall see in a later chapter, he was drowned in the sea at Le Havre just before the end of the war.

As cable technology improved and as greater capacity was required, new cables were laid. In 1913 *The Times* reported that a new cable had been laid between Abergeirch and Howth near Dublin by the Post Office cable ship *Monarch*. The report goes on to say that 'this has made a notable addition to the telephonic facilities' with Ireland.[4] Two more new telephone cables were laid between Abergeirch and Howth by the Cable Ship *Faraday* in 1937 and 1938. Before the Second World War broke out a new fully-automated repeater station was established in Morfa village and the manually-operated relay office became redundant.

Lloyd George, the Nefyn Fishermen and the By-Election of 1890

At an early age David Lloyd George became interested in politics. In 1886, aged just 23, he sought the Liberal nomination for the Merioneth seat but he subsequently withdrew. Two years later, in 1888, this fiery, ambitious, young solicitor was successful in gaining the Liberal Party nomination for the Caernarfon Boroughs seat, which was then held for the Tories by Edmund Swetenham, a wealthy landowning barrister. Lloyd George's moment arrived much sooner than he expected, for in 1890 Swetenham died unexpectedly, following a fall from his horse during fox hunting. A by-election would have to be held.

But the young solicitor was facing a number of problems. Firstly, Members of Parliament were unpaid (they did not receive a salary until 1911), so initially Lloyd George had to rely for finance on the family legal practice which he had set up with his brother, William. Previously, the seat for the Caernarfon Boroughs had always been held by influential wealthy landowners. Lloyd George was neither wealthy nor influential, and politically he was a radical Liberal. His unorthodox views caused him to be viewed with contempt by Tory supporters and with a considerable suspicion by the more moderate Gladstonian elements within his own party. Furthermore, he was young and relatively unknown, although he had achieved some notoriety locally as the solicitor who had won the much-publicised Llanfrothen burial case.

His problems were compounded by the composition of the electorate within the Caernarfon Boroughs, for there were strong Conservative forces present. Bangor, with its Anglican cathedral and three Conservative Clubs, was a bastion of Conservatism. Caernarfon had a Conservative Working

Men's Club, an Anglican Training College, four Anglican churches, a militia barracks and 45 taverns – hardly fertile electoral ground for a Liberal Nonconformist advocating temperance and Welsh nationalism. In previous elections Conwy had also revealed a substantial body of Tory voters. It was clear that Lloyd George would have to depend for his support upon the smaller, solidly Welsh-speaking boroughs of Cricieth, Nefyn and Pwllheli.

But even in those smaller, intensely Welsh boroughs there were difficulties. At both Cricieth and Pwllhei there was a substantial Tory element, while in Nefyn there were several taverns and a flourishing Conservative Club. Furthermore, it must be remembered that there were still no universal voting rights, for the electorate consisted mainly of the more affluent middle classes. The 1890 Nefyn electoral register is not available, but the register for 1891 reveals that out of a total Nefyn population of nearly 1,800 only 366 people were entitled to vote. On that list there was a preponderance of middle class businessmen, men from the professions, small artisan employers, farmers and a number of skilled working men. It was clear that Lloyd George would have to appeal to the middle class Nonconformists for his support. However, not all Nonconformists would support him. During the 1890 election one observer commented that the majority of Nefyn Baptists were Tories, and at his first campaign meeting at the Madryn Hall it was noted that there was not a single Baptist in the audience, despite the fact that Lloyd George himself was a Baptist. It has also been suggested that some Nefyn folk voted Tory because so many of the English visitors coming to the town were Church-going, Tory folk.

Ironically, Lloyd George's Tory opponent at the 1890 by-election was Hugh Ellis Nanney who owned most of the Llanystumdwy area where Lloyd George had grown up as a child. Fearing that his views were being regarded as too extreme, Lloyd George began to tone down his speeches so that he might appeal to as wide an audience as possible. Needless to say, he was subsequently pilloried by his opponents for back-tracking on his manifesto. On the eve of the poll the result seemed to be in the balance.

The voting on polling day was extremely heavy, the highest ever in the constituency. But the result could scarcely have been closer. At the end of the day, following a recount, Lloyd George was declared the winner by just 18 votes.

This slender margin prompted the Tory newspaper *Y Gwalia* to suggest that Lloyd George had only managed to win the seat because a severe storm at sea, which had lasted for two days, had prevented a host of Tory-voting Nefyn fishermen from coming ashore to cast their votes!

This by-election success was the start of a glittering career for the young lawyer. Lloyd George was to represent the Caernarfon Boroughs for 54 years, and he was destined to become President of the Board of Trade and Chancellor of the Exchequer. During the Great War he was to perform vital roles as Minister for Munitions, then Secretary of State for War and finally Prime Minister, a position which he held until 1922.

If the view expressed in *Y Gwalia* was correct then the Tory-voting fishermen of Nefyn, by their enforced absence, had inadvertently changed the course of history!

The First Nefyn Show 1891
Since the early 1890s one of the highlights of the year at Nefyn has been the Nefyn Show, or the Llŷn and District Agricultural Show, to give it its official title. Henry Parry records that the first Nefyn Show was held in 1891[5], and the following year the *North Wales Chronicle* announced that the 'Lleyn Horse Dog and Poultry Show' was to be held at Nefyn on Easter Monday 'with £100 to be awarded in prizes'.[6]

The Nefyn Show used to be known locally as the Easter Horse Show or the 'Mownti', and a newspaper report of 1893 reported that there were 24 classes for the horse judging.[7] Although the show was not exclusive to horses it must be remembered that horse power was extremely important during the 19th century before the advent of mechanisation. It was the horse which pulled the farm plough and the wagon; it pulled the coach and the trap; and some people travelled around the area on horseback.

As a child, immediately after the Great War, John Ifor Davies remembered the Mownti being held in Cae John Bull, a field situated between Saint David's Church and Caeau Capel. Two or three days before the show farmers would flock into the town with their livestock to be accommodated temporarily at Tŷ Cerrig and other suitable premises which possessed outbuildings.

Lloyd George was a frequent visitor to the Nefyn Show. R. Gerallt Jones, in his book, recalled the former Prime Minister's visit to the Nefyn Show in either 1939 or 1940. He remembered seeing Lloyd George's 'car rolling in, and the uniformed chauffeur coming out and opening the car boot and turning it into a speaker's rostrum. The old man, white hair streaming in the wind, mounted the platform, stick in hand, and began to speak.'

For more than a century the Nefyn Show was held on Easter Monday, and it was always the earliest of the local shows. In 2001 it was not possible to hold the show on account of the foot and mouth outbreak. Instead, a rally of old vehicles was held on the field at Bryn Mynach beside Saint Mary's Church. Thankfully, the Nefyn Show has now resumed although it is currently held each May Bank Holiday.

Today the Nefyn Show takes place on the fields of Botacho Wyn, near Y Bryncynan, and it provides competition classes for horses, cattle, sheep, smaller animals and poultry as well as cookery and craftwork. It also includes an exhibition of old cars and farm equipment, various trade stands, refreshments, a number of displays and a fun fair for the children. Each May Bank Holiday farmers from all over Llŷn and beyond come to Nefyn to exhibit their livestock, and the show, which has a very distinctive local atmosphere, is an occasion when people of all ages can enjoy a thoroughly entertaining day out. The veteran and vintage vehicle show, which is still held each Easter Monday, provides a rare opportunity for people to see some classic vehicles from the past.

An 'Invasion' of Nefyn
Many years ago there was a belief in Llŷn that one day the Irish would invade the Welsh mainland, and it was a tradition which persisted at the end of the 19th century. Several stories are told of desperate and dishevelled shipwrecked mariners, knocking on the doors of remote Llŷn cottages and farmsteads in the middle of the night, only to be mistaken for invading Irishmen. When rumours of such an invasion were rife Llŷn people would lock and bar their doors after dark. Nobody knows how such rumours originated, for the Irish had not invaded the peninsula since the Dark Ages!

There is an amusing story told by Tomos Jones[8] who was born in about 1879 on a 15 acre farm called Tŷ Newydd on Ynys Enlli (*Bardsey Island*). Tomos recounted how one day the men of Enlli took to their boats to go fishing in Nefyn Bay. They were wearing their traditional fishing gear – clogs on their feet, clothes dipped in coal tar to afford protection against the salt water and small round hats on their heads. They also wore long dark beards which obscured their faces.

Eventually the Enlli fishermen ran their boats onto the beach at Nefyn so that they could go into the town to buy some food. But as soon as the local folk saw those terrifying figures walking along the street towards them they ran off in a panic, yelling 'The Irish have come! Run for your lives!'

Undeterred, the Enlli men made their way to one of the shops. However, as soon as the shopkeeper saw them stepping across her threshold she screamed, 'Oh dear! The Irish have come! You can take anything you want, but please spare my life.' The visitors explained that they were not Irish, but they were simply fishermen from Enlli who had come to buy food.

'Oh dear! I thought you were the Irish!' the shopkeeper stammered, still trembling like a leaf.

The Building of the Madryn Hall 1898

The building of the Madryn Hall (so named after the nearby Madryn Castle, the ancestral home of the Jones Parry family) was commenced in 1898, when the foundation stone was laid by Love Jones Parry's wife. The official opening of the Hall took place during the following year, and over the succeeding years the Madryn Hall was used for a variety of purposes from political meetings to concerts, plays, dances and films.

It was in the Madryn Hall that, on numerous occasions, Lloyd George addressed the people of Nefyn when he was campaigning for the Caernarfon Boroughs seat. We are told that, on such occasions, the place would be overflowing, and that every seat would be taken. People would be crowding in the doorways and sitting on the window ledges. As he spoke, the audience would hang on his every word, and his speech would be interrupted at regular intervals by thunderous applause and roars of approval. Such was the power of his oratory.

Henry Parry records that, before the Great War, a small basement room in the Madryn Hall was set aside as the Gazette Room where the *Shipping Gazette* was always on display. Local folk would go to the Gazette Room to follow the movement of the ships on which their loved ones were sailing. It was also the place where old mariners and sea captains would gather to smoke their pipes and share their tales of rounding the Horn or their exploits in far-off foreign ports.

Concerts and plays were performed in the Hall, too. John Ifor Davies remembered the 'Annual Concert for Visitors' being held in the Madryn Hall each summer between the two World Wars. Later, plays written by the local children's author, Elizabeth Watkin-Jones, were performed in the hall by the children of Capel Soar. Moreover, it was in the Madryn Hall that films were shown between the two world wars, and forty or fifty years ago summer visitors recollect going there on a Sunday evening for community hymn singing, accompanied by the Nefyn Town Band. The Madryn Hall was also the place where, each summer, the Rose Queen was crowned, in front of a packed audience.

During the Second World War the Madryn Hall was commandeered by the Government for military use. In May 1941 disaster almost befell the building. The *Caernarfon and Denbigh Herald* records that, early one morning in May 1941, 'flames were seen issuing from the roof of the Madryn Hall. The fire brigade was summoned and they arrived on the scene very promptly. The firemen got the fire under control in a short time and only light damage was caused.'[9] In 1945 the Madryn Hall, which had been released from war use by the military, was renovated and repainted. It was then adopted as the official Nefyn Town Hall, 'the town's coat of arms having been transferred there from the Old Town Hall in Stryd Fawr.'[10]

Towards the end of the 20th century the old Madryn Hall, which was no longer in use, became dilapidated and derelict. As it lay abandoned, a new *Canolfan* was built on the Morfa Road, although that building has since been demolished to be replaced by a brand new, 21st century community hall which was constructed on the same site in 2010. The old Madryn Hall was demolished in 2006. Whilst the new building is to be welcomed as an excellent, state-of-the-art community facility it is rather sad to think that the historic old Neuadd Madryn has completely disappeared. For nearly 100 years it had been at the heart of so much of Nefyn's history, and it still conjures up many happy memories for visitors and older residents alike.

Nefyn Football Club, late 19th Century – Present
It seems that a Nefyn football team was in existence as early as the late 1890's when local quarryman, John Parry, 'the grand old man of Nefyn' who lived to be 100 years of age, was a member of the team.[11] He is also recorded as a player during the 1904-5 season when the Nefyn team was competing against teams like Pwllheli, Porthmadog and Penygroes. The players were all local lads, mainly seamen and quarry workers. A photograph[12] of the team records the names of the players – Robert Jones, P. R. Owen (Gwalia Café), Edward Evans (Tŷ Llewelyn), John Parry (Sea View, Tai Lon), John Henry Baum, Tom Hughes, Hugh Williams (Bodeuon), Richard Griffith Jones and the three Cooke brothers (The Revd T. A. Cooke, who was the vicar of Cricieth, David F. Cooke and George Cooke). Accompanying the team on the photograph were Mr R. A. Naylor, Cliff Castle, who stood as a Tory candidate against Lloyd George a few years later, and Mr Davies, assistant master at the Nefyn School. Apparently the 1904-5 season ended in an unusual and rather dramatic manner. Having been gripped by the Great Religious Revival of that year, the players disbanded the team, dug a deep hole in the ground and ceremoniously buried their football![13]

By 1909 the Nefyn team had been re-formed, for it comprised R. Jones, H. Jones Hughes, D. Hughes, W. Jones, R. Thomas, Robert Jones, R. Wilson, G. Cooke, John Ellis, W. Jones and R. Griffith.[14] The team must have been disbanded during the 1914-18 war, since many of its members would have been conscripted into the army. A Nefyn football team was in existence again during the 1920's, for there is a photograph of the team, dated 1926, in the Gwynedd Archives,[15] and by the 1932-33 season the 'Nevin Celts' were playing in the Bangor League. Since many of the team's opponents were from the Bangor area or even further afield, travelling must have been very time-consuming and fairly tiring. At the end of that season 'The Celts' finished bottom of the league.

Prior to 1937-38 they joined the 'Lleyn & District League' playing against teams like Cricieth, Sarn, Cooke's United and Pwllheli Reserves. Their football pitch was Holborn Field. For the duration of the Second World War the Nefyn team was disbanded again. The Nefyn Celts were re-formed in 1945 when they played in the Third Caernarfonshire League.[16] At the start of the 1947-48 season they rejoined the Bangor & District League in which they finished fourth. R. O. Jones, Nant y Felin, had the honour of being selected to play for the Bangor & District Representative side in February 1950.[17]

At the end of the 1949-50 season the Nefyn team played in the Caernarfon and District League. The years 1952-1955 constituted a golden period for the Nefyn team because they won the league and all the cups. From 1957 to 1960 the team did not play owing to financial difficulties, but they took part in the Caernarfon and District League again in 1961. They remained in that league until they were promoted to the Gwynedd League in 1987.

For three seasons, from 1991, they played in the Fitlock League, but had to resign owing to a lack of players. In 2000 the Nefyn club won the Junior Cup for the first time in its history, and the team was promoted once more to the Gwynedd League. In 2004 Nefyn United won the John Smith Cup by beating Bangor University on penalties in the final. In 2005 they were promoted from the Gwynedd League to the Alliance League where they finished runners up, and during the seasons 2005-6 & 2006-7 the team enjoyed very good cup runs. In 2008-9 they finished 7th in the League and were semi-finalists in the Welsh Trophy.

The club ground is Cae'r Delyn which is situated near Y Bryncynan. The club also runs a reserve team which plays in the Gwynedd Safeflue League and Junior teams which play in the Llŷn and Eifionydd League.

Notes

1. Sutton's North Wales Directory 1889-90
2. Caernarvonshire & Angelsey Postal Directory 1886
3. C&DH 11/08/1893
4. *Times* 30/12/1913
5. Henry Parry Papers – Gwynedd Archives (X/M/804/38)
6. NWC 09/04/1892
7. C&DH 07/04/1893
8. Story told in *Tomos the Islandman* by Jennie Jones
9. C&DH 23/05/1941

10 *C&DH* 13/07/1945
11 Photograph in 'Straeon am Nefyn' by Dr Brian Owen on internet site Nefyn.com
12 Photograph of the team – Gwynedd Archives (X/CHS/1274/11/13)
13 *C&DH* 17/02/1939
14 Photograph of the players – Gwynedd Archives (X/CHS.1279/12/1)
15 Photograph of the team – Gwynedd Archives (X/CHS.1279/11/121)
16 *C&DH* 09/11/1945
17 *C&DH* 24/02/1950

Chapter 2

The Early 20th Century 1900-1914

Introduction
In the years leading up to the Great War, Nefyn and the surrounding district remained a farming, fishing, quarrying and maritime region. The numerous farms in the parish continued to provide employment for large numbers of local men and boys, and a sale of livestock was held annually by Messrs J. Parry Jones at the Bryncynan Inn.[1] In the early 1900s there were 40 fishing boats working from Porth Nefyn, the granite quarries were booming, and the two communities of Nefyn and Morfa Nefyn still provided numerous sea captains and sailors to man the merchant fleet.

But the days of sail were fading, and the majority of seamen were now pursuing careers on the steam-powered vessels which belonged to the large shipping companies, based in major ports such as Liverpool, London, Cardiff and Newcastle. However, there were still some Nefyn seafarers who preferred to serve on the sailing barques and fully-rigged ships belonging to the large Welsh sailing fleets, like that of Robert Thomas & Company of Liverpool. As J. Ifor Davies recalls, there was a great deal of light-hearted banter between those sailors still under sail and those who had moved into steam, the two factions frequently directing terms like 'windbag' and 'steam kettle' at one another!

A few local master mariners had moved to live in Liverpool, but Nefyn and Morfa village remained home to a large number of locally-born ships' captains and sailors. Wealthy master mariners built large imposing houses for themselves and their families, and the Morfa Road became the most desirable residential area in Nefyn. Sea captains now tended to purchase shares in the large shipping companies rather than buying 'ounces' in locally-owned vessels.

The granite quarries continued to employ a considerable number of men from Nefyn and the surrounding area. At its height between 1900 and 1904 the Gwylwyr Quarry employed over 100 men, although production virtually ceased with the outbreak of the Great War. The Bodeilias Quarry employed 84 workers in 1901, but the quarry had closed by 1907. The Dywyrch Quarry closed in 1903 and the brickworks at Bwlch, Morfa Nefyn, ceased production in about 1906.

During the same year a new reservoir was constructed on Mynydd

Nefyn to provide a piped water supply to the town. Steam coasters continued to arrive at Porth Dinllaen, bringing essential goods and supplies for distribution to shops and farms across the northern part of Llŷn. Seaborne coal was brought regularly to the beaches at both Porth Nefyn and Porth Dinllaen, for coal was still the fuel by which people heated their homes and cooked their meals. The paraffin lamp was the principal source of lighting.

The last great religious revival swept through Wales in 1904-5, and it coincided with the building of Saint David's Anglican Church and the Seion Baptist Chapel, both in 1904. In that year the chapel congregations in particular were gripped by an intense religious fervour which focused upon the spiritual aspects of life and which soundly rejected many of the material things of this world. As Morgan and Thomas so aptly put it 'the Great Revival of 1904-5 was an attempt to return the Welsh people to the Puritan certainties of an earlier age.' The dynamic young South Wales evangelist, Evan Roberts, visited Llŷn in December 1904, preaching at both Pwllheli and Nefyn during that year. For a short time the effects of the revival were quite dramatic. However, the intensity and the zeal which it generated did not last for very long.

In 1902 Board schools were taken over by local education authorities, and the Nefyn Board School now became Nefyn Council School. It continued to be an all age school where children remained until they reached the age of 13. In 1908 a new school was established in Morfa Nefyn, although part way through their education Morfa children were required to transfer to the Nefyn School where they remained until they attained the statutory school leaving age. During the early years of the century an Englishman, Mr Laurence Hart, established a girls' school for both boarders and day pupils at Plas Tirion. It was called the Morfa Nefyn College for Girls, and it concentrated upon good behaviour, deportment, character training, a Christian education and a range of outdoor sports and activities. However, the college did not seem to be a great success since it only lasted for about three or four years.

The early years of the 20th century ushered in the first sightings of motorised transport in the Nefyn area, although horse-drawn coaches were still operating, and many farmers continued to travel around the area by pony and trap. In 1906 the Cambrian Railway Company purchased a pair of two cylinder 16 horse power omnibuses with solid tyres and seating for 22 passengers. These omnibuses operated a service between Pwllheli, Nefyn, Morfa Nefyn and Edern. During the next year a Morfa Nefyn horse-drawn coaching company purchased an omnibus and started to operate a rival service on four days of the week. Soon afterwards Owen Parry established the 'Nevin and District Omnibus Company' in opposition to the other two firms. But just before the outbreak of the Great War the Nefyn and Morfa omnibus companies amalgamated so that they were better able to compete with the larger Cambrian Company.

The Nefyn golf club was founded in 1907, and when the Morfa Nefyn brickyard chimney was subsequently demolished the rubble from it was used to create a foundation for the road leading to the new golf course. Also during 1907 the Nefyn Post Office became an independent sub-office. During these years the area continued to grow in importance as a holiday destination, and it was during this period that additional development took place along the road leading to Morfa Nefyn, including the building of several Edwardian villa-style properties. In the years preceeding the outbreak of the Great War, more and more Nefyn people began taking in visitors as paying guests during the season. Just before the outbreak of the Great War the new Nanhoron Arms Hotel was built opposite Saint David's Church, and further unsuccessful attempts were made to bring the railway to Nefyn and Porth Dinllaen. In May 1902 a new lifeboat arrived at the Porth Dinllaen station. Called the *Barbara Fleming*, she was a 12-oared, self righting boat like her predecessors.

Immediately prior to 1900 Britain had embarked upon a second war with the South African Boer republics of the Transvaal and the Orange Free State, a war which Lloyd George vehemently denounced. Although his views brought him a great deal of notoriety in British politics, they caused the majority of people, including many of his own Nefyn constituents, to brand him a traitor.

For many Nefyn folk at this time, the reasons to travel were few. Apart from mariners, who travelled widely, and others like carriers, who undertook journeys in connection with their daily work, many local people would seldom have needed to venture beyond the borders of their own parish. Whenever they did cross the parish boundary it would be to go to a nearby town or to visit relatives or friends in a neighbouring village.

When the Great War broke out, several of the parish's young men left the security of their Nefyn and Morfa Nefyn homes to join the army. In a short space of time they would be suffering the dangers and privations of life in the trenches on the Western Front, in the Balkans or in the Middle East. Tragically, a considerable number of them would never return home. Many local master mariners and seamen were also destined to lose their lives during this conflict, mainly as a result of their ships being torpedoed by enemy submarines.

Lloyd George, the People of Nefyn and the Boer War

In October 1899, when war broke out between South African Boers (who were of Dutch ancestry) and the British Government, Lloyd George championed the Boers, since he viewed their cause as a struggle for survival by a small nation against a mighty empire.

It was Lloyd George's forthright support for the Boers which propelled him from virtual obscurity to prominence in British politics. In the House of Commons he spoke out passionately against the war. He denounced it as an unjust war being fought on behalf of greedy Rand gold mining interests in the homeland of the Boers. He also attacked the burning of Boer farmsteads and the imprisonment of Boer women and children.

Such a stance was particularly courageous since there was a great deal of wholehearted support for this war among the mass of the ordinary people. Even in his own county of Caernarfonshire he was pilloried for his pro-Boer stance. The *North Wales Chronicle* suggested that Lloyd George's criticism was tantamount to treason. 'Mr Lloyd George's speech is the shame of Caernarvonshire' and 'a shock to the feeling of nine out of ten of his constituents' it suggested.[2] 'The overruling majority of his registered supporters are against Mr Lloyd George and the pro-Boer advocacy,' the paper subsequently declared.[3]

It is not surprising that a popular fury was unleashed against Lloyd George, even by his own people. Welsh troops had been sent to South Africa, and local sailors and sea captains were transporting men and supplies to the Cape. For example, Captain Henry Parry, Caerau, (the father of Henry Parry, the Nefyn dentist) was master of the *SS Monterey* which transported troops to South Africa. So unpopular were Lloyd George's views that, when he attempted to address a meeting at the Penrhyn Hall, Bangor, he came close to being lynched by a frenzied mob which he later described as being 'seized with a drunken madness'. Everywhere Lloyd George went he was denounced. Even the people of Nefyn, Cricieth and Pwllheli, three towns upon which he depended for his political support, became so hostile that effigies of him, his brother William, and his Uncle Richard, were burned in public.

In an article entitled 'Reminiscences of Mr Lloyd George', which subsequently appeared in the *North Wales Chronicle*, R. O. Fadog described Lloyd George's visit to Nefyn for a public meeting during the early part of the war:

> One dark and wet November evening Mr Lloyd George was to hold a meeting at Nevin and he gave me a lift from Pwllheli. Alderman W. Eifl

Jones and Mrs George were with us. I anticipated trouble at Nevin, but before we reached the town, just at the top of the steep hill that leads to High Street, we were pelted with sods. When we got to the hall a hostile crowd met us at the entrance, and during the holding of the meeting frequent interruptions took place. Mr Lloyd George, however, braved the opposition smilingly. On the way back we were again attacked at the very same place.[4]

R. O. Fadog went on to point out that Lloyd George held other meetings at both Nefyn and Pwllheli prior to the 1900 election, and that 'by sheer force of his eloquence and his personality he captured the majority of voters in both towns.' By this time the jingoistic support for the war, which had existed at the outset, had waned considerably. Furthermore, although this election was dominated by the South African war (it became known as 'The Khaki War'), Lloyd George skilfully sidestepped that issue, preferring to campaign on those Welsh matters which affected his constituents most urgently.

Following that election in the autumn of 1900, Lloyd George was returned to Parliament by his constituents with his largest majority to date – 296 votes. It seems that his cause was greatly assisted by the fact that his Tory opponent was a certain Colonel Platt, a military man who could speak no Welsh, who showed little commitment to Welsh affairs and who has been described as a 'mild-mannered nonentity.'

Nevertheless, it is remarkable to think that within the space of a few years Lloyd George's reputation would be transformed, not only in Nefyn but right across Wales and the whole of Britain, from that of traitor who opposed the government during the Boer War to hero and Prime Minister who led the British people to victory during the Great War.

Two More Attempts to Bring the Railway to Nefyn and Porth Dinllaen

In 1900 a group of local people made another attempt to link Nefyn and Porth Dinllaen to the rail network when they put forward plans for the 'Nevin and Porthdinllaen Light Railway.' It was envisaged that a new section of the line would extend from Pwllheli along the coast beyond Penrhos before turning northwards and continuing to Porth Dinllaen, with a subsidiary line to Nefyn branching off between Boduan and Y Bryncynan. Once again the necessary investment did not materialise.

In 1913 the Cambrian Railway Company made yet another attempt to take the railway to the northern coast of Llŷn. This attempt also failed to get off the ground because the war with Germany broke out. But even if the war had not intervened it is doubtful if the project would have gone ahead, for there was no longer any need for another significant coastal port. At this time, throughout Wales, the railways were the important means by which goods were moved around the country, locally the roads had improved and consequently the coastal sea trade was in decline. Never again would anyone consider trying to transform Porth Dinllaen into an important port.

A Nefyn Sailor's Bravery during a Foreign Earthquake 1905

In September 1905 17 year old Evan Davies, who was the son of Captain and Mrs Davies, Terfyn and who later became well known as Captain Evan Davies, Hafan, was on board his ship which had docked in the harbour at Messina, Sicily. The port of Messina, occupying an important position on the narrow strait between Sicily and the 'toe' of the Italian mainland, was a significant trading port with an excellent harbour. The *Caernarfon and Denbigh Herald*[5] subsequently reported, in an extremely understated manner, that Evan Davies had a 'thrilling experience' whilst his ship was in that port.

The report goes on to state that at 01.43 am on 8th September 1905 there occurred a violent earthquake with a magnitude of approximately 6.9 on the scale. Enormous damage was inflicted on Calabria (the region on the toe of Italy) with 25 villages obliterated, 600 persons killed, 2000 injured and 300,000 made homeless. At Messina the ships in the harbour were suddenly hit by a massive tidal wave which lifted them bodily out of the water, hurling them around in total chaos. The force of that wave was so great that it breached the harbour wall, and during the confusion that followed, young Evan Davies assisted in rescuing 34 people from drowning. For his bravery the young Morfa Nefyn sailor was awarded a silver medal and a diploma by the King of Italy.

The Building of a Reservoir for Nefyn 1906

As has been previously mentioned, for centuries the people of Nefyn had been forced to rely upon Saint Mary's well for their water supply. During the 19th century several Caernarfonshire towns had experienced outbreaks of cholera, caused by contaminated wells and springs, and as a consequence some towns, including Bangor, Caernarfon, Pwllheli, Cricieth and Porthmadog, had installed purpose-built reservoirs and piped water. However, by the turn of the century, Nefyn residents were still relying upon Saint Mary's well.

In January 1899 it was reported by Doctor Thomas of the 'Lleyn District Council' that the local authority was 'moving forward to get a proper water supply to Nevin', and that an engineer had been 'engaged to look into the matter'.⁶ The Nefyn reservoir was completed in 1906, having been hewn from the granite rock on Mynydd Nefyn, from where water was piped down into the town. A Nefyn Water Committee was formed to oversee all matters concerning the new water supply, and the reservoir was officially opened by David Lloyd George. During his speech at the opening ceremony Lloyd George quipped, 'Henceforth the people of Nefyn will be able to say, "I have drunk water from the rock!"'.

This auspicious occasion in Nefyn's history was marked by great celebrations. A procession of local school children marched through the town led by the Nefyn Town Band, and this was followed by a water display on Y Groes, performed by firemen from Pwllheli.

The Founding of Nefyn Golf Club 1907

In 1907 a group of local men convened a meeting at the Tŷ Coch Inn, Porth Dinllaen, where they took the decision to lay out a nine hole golf course on Penrhyn Porth Dinllaen, the long narrow headland which extends into the sea. And so the Nefyn Golf Club was born. The first club house, a wooden structure with a thatched roof, was built in 1909 but it was burnt down the following year.

In 1912 the course was extended to form an 18 hole course of 5,000 yards, and in 1913 a road was constructed from Penrhos, Morfa Nefyn, to the golf course. The replacement club house, another wooden building, was also burnt down in 1928.

In the 1920s and 1930s the course was developed further under the guidance of two well known golf course architects, James Braid (the famous Scottish golf professional) and John Henry Taylor (the renowned English professional golfer). Each had won the British Open on five occasions. Taylor described the Nefyn course as 'situated on one of the most beautiful sites I have ever seen.' Henry Parry records that the present clubhouse was built in 1930. In 1933 additional holes were added to the existing 18 hole course.

Many famous names have played on the Nefyn course. Clement Attlee, the post-war Labour Prime Minister, played here many times when he was staying in Nefyn. Others have included Dai Rees (captain of the Ryder Cup winning team in 1957), Ronan Rafferty (Ryder Cup winner, golf commentator and analyst), Peter Allis (Ryder Cup player and golf commentator), Brian Huggett (Ryder Cup player six times and non-playing captain in 1977), Mike Atherton (former England cricket captain) and Ian Woosnam (nine times winner of the Ryder Cup and winner of the US Masters).

Today the Nefyn course is a unique 26 hole championship course with stunning scenery, and delightful views of the sea from every tee. One can look across to Yr Eifl and Anglesey, while there are also fine views of the Snowdon range. If the visibility is clear one can see the Wicklow Mountains in southern Ireland. It is not surprising that, for many decades, a walk across the golf course has been a favourite pastime for visitors to the area.

Golfers from all over the world, including America, Japan and Scandinavia, have visited Nefyn to sample the delights of this course, often visiting it as part of a European golf tour. For several successive years, golfing enthusiasts have voted the Nefyn course one of the top 100 golf courses in the United Kingdom.[7]

After playing the first ten holes, golfers can either choose to play the newer holes or they can head out onto the headland to play the original holes which are bounded by sheer cliffs above a rocky coastline and the sandy beach at Porth Dinllaen. The holes on this narrow promontory hug the cliff edge, and many a golfer has driven a succession of balls into the sea. In the summer of 2005 when Seasearch divers carried out a survey of marine species and their habitats in the sea around Porth Dinllaen they discovered not only interesting marine plants and sea creatures but also scores of golf balls!

There is a story told that, several years ago, one golfer sliced ten balls in quick succession over the edge of the cliff. He was so angry and frustrated that he stomped to the cliff edge and hurled his bag of clubs into the water. Then, muttering under his breath, he marched off to the club house to drown his sorrows. A fairly costly round of golf one would suspect!

The Opening of Morfa Nefyn School 1908

In 1908 the village of Morfa Nefyn was granted its own school so that young children no longer had to walk to the schools at Nefyn or Edern each day. The building, which was erected as a temporary structure, consisted of a wooden framework clad in corrugated iron and topped by a corrugated iron roof. The corrugated iron was always painted in a very distinctive shade of red. Tom Morris, who was a pupil at the school, recollects that the accommodation comprised two classrooms, two cloakrooms, toilets and two stone-built shelters to the rear, and a coal shed adjacent to the road. The classrooms were heated by two large coal-fired stoves and the building was able to accommodate 80 pupils. Outside near the main entrance hung a bell which was rung to announce the start of school. If children heard that bell ringing when they were on the way to school they knew that they were going to be in trouble for being late.

Under its head, Miss Grace A. Roberts, the new school opened for the first time on Monday 2nd November, 1908 and 59 children attended. Two years later an HMI report on the school stated that the building, although of a temporary nature, was 'well adapted for teaching purposes' and was 'a comfortable one in which to work in both summer and winter.' It went on to state that the children 'are most carefully taught and are making creditable progress.' The report also praised the school's equipment which included a piano, funded partly from local subscriptions and partly out of a Local Authority grant. For over 100 years Ysgol Morfa Nefyn has served generations of young Morfa children very well indeed.

But, as often happens with things that are supposed to be of a temporary nature, the original wood and corrugated iron structure became semi-permanent, for it was not replaced with a brick building until 1982. The original 'temporary' school building had remained in service for 74 years!

An Unusual Lifeboat Accident at Porth Dinllaen 1913

On Wednesday November 13th 1913 there occurred an unusual lifeboat accident at the Porth Dinllaen station, and the victim was 55 year old William Thomas of Gerallt, Nefyn. He was the son of John Thomas, the influential Nefyn shipowner, and the grandson of John John Thomas, the famous early Nefyn shipbuilder, both of whom have been mentioned already.

William Thomas did not follow in the family tradition of a career at sea, but instead he went to work for the 'Carnarvonshire District Bank'. In due course, he was promoted to the position of manager of the branch in Bangor. When he retired he returned to Nefyn to live at Gerallt, next door to the old family home, Iorwerth. He became a committee member of the Porth Dinllaen lifeboat, a Justice of the Peace and Treasurer of the Nefyn Golf Club.

As a Porth Dinllaen Lifeboat Committee member he often assisted at practice launches. The *Caernarfon and Denbigh Herald*[8] records that, during one such launch in November 1913, William Thomas was in the *Barbara Fleming* as she slid down the slipway. During the descent he thought that a quarter stopper (a rope designed to check the speed of the boat as it slid towards the sea) was uncoiling too quickly, so he put his left boot on it to slow it down. Unfortunately the rope wrapped itself around his ankle just above the boot, completely wrenching his foot off.

Sadly William Thomas had experienced an even greater tragedy earlier in his life. In the very year that he became manager of the bank in Bangor he married his wife Margaret Jane, but the following year his young wife died in childbirth and the baby died too.

William Thomas died in 1937 at the age of 79, and he was buried in the same grave in Glanadda Cemetery, Bangor, where his young wife and infant had been buried 50 years earlier. Many well-known county folk attended his funeral including Margaret Lloyd George, wife of the former British Prime Minister.

A Fatal Accident at the Gwylwyr Quarry 1914

On 16th May, 1914, a few months before the outbreak of the Great War, a sudden fall of rock at the Gwylwyr Quarry killed a 40 year old local worker, Mr William Mona Hughes Town Hall, who was a native of Llanerchymedd, Anglesey. William Hughes not only worked at the quarry, but he and his wife also kept a cycle shop at Town Hall, Stryd Fawr, a business which William's wife, Jane, continued to run after her husband's death. Ifor Davies recalls how, upon hearing of Mr Hughes's fatal accident, the entire town was so shocked that it was almost as if a cloud had descended over the entire place, and for a while people went about talking in whispers. Little did everyone realise that, within a short space of time once the Great War had started, other Nefyn families would be experiencing, with sickening regularity, the same kind of grief which Mrs Jane Hughes and her children were feeling.

Notes
[1] C&DH 13/10/1907
[2] NWC 04/11/1899
[3] NWC 09/12/1899
[4] NWC 15/12/1916
[5] C&DH 01/01/1943
[6] C&DH 13/01/1899
[7] 'Golf International' awarded the Nefyn course 83rd place in 'Britain's Top 100 Courses' 2003
[8] C&DH 21/11/1913

Chapter 3

The Great War 1914-18

Introduction
When war broke out in the summer of 1914 it was supposed to be 'the war to end all wars', and many anticipated that the fighting would be over by Christmas. Few people could have predicted the slaughter and the mayhem that was to follow. Efficient modern weapons like the belt-fed machine gun which could pump out bullets at the rate of ten per second, the magazine rifle, long range heavy artillery, U-boats, mines, torpedoes, tanks, flying machines and poisonous gas were all to contribute to the hideous destruction and death toll.

Military tactics on the Western Front were suicidal. Following an intense artillery bombardment of enemy positions, masses of troops were required to go 'over the top' with bayonets fixed, and then charge across 'no-man's land' to storm the opposing trenches. Many were cut down by rapid fire as they charged forward. Those who reached the enemy lines were forced to embark upon ferocious hand-to-hand fighting in the hope of securing a few miserable yards of barren muddy ground, pitted with shell holes. The deadly fire power of the latest hand-held weapons placed the odds firmly in favour of the defending troops, although the blast and shrapnel from a high explosive shell, exploding within the confines of a trench, could kill and fatally injure many soldiers. Consequently a whole generation of young men, including many from the parish of Nefyn, were destined to be killed, maimed and psychologically traumatised during this conflict.

From the outset, Welsh opinion about the war was divided. The majority of Welsh people put aside their traditional Liberal pacifism and accepted the war as a just cause. They saw it as a struggle fought on behalf of little nations, and 'Poor little Belgium' (which had been invaded by the German Kaiser) had a popular appeal for many Welsh folk. Even some Welsh ministers of religion played their part in boosting army recruitment.

Lloyd George, Member of Parliament for Nefyn and the other Caernarfon Boroughs, wrote to his wife in August 1914, 'I am moving through a nightmare world these days.' All his instincts were against war with Germany, as they had been against war with the Boers in 1899. However, despite his opposition to the war, Lloyd George decided not to resign from the Government. His initial scepticism about this conflict very soon gave way to wholehearted involvement when he became Minister of Munitions (May 1915), Secretary of State for War (May 1916) and finally Prime Minister (Dec 1916). Many Nefyn and Morfa men were caught up in this conflict both on land and at sea, but the inhabitants of the parish must have felt even more closely involved in the war effort, since their Member of Parliament was occupying such high profile Government posts. There is no doubt that the important wartime offices of state held by Lloyd George greatly boosted people's support for the war right across Wales.

Nevertheless, there were some Welsh Nonconformists and Nationalists who opposed the war fervently, either as a matter of conscience or on the grounds that this conflict had nothing to do with the Welsh nation. As time went by, news of the mass slaughter in the trenches, together with the introduction of conscription, added to the number of Welsh voices crying out in opposition.

From the start, aided by a concerted recruitment campaign launched by Lord Kitchener, the Secretary of State for War, large numbers of Welshmen enthusiastically volunteered to join the army, including men from Nefyn. In proportion to population, more Welshmen took part in the Great War than either Englishmen or Scotsmen. But so heavy were the casualties during the first 18 months of the conflict that it soon became obvious that victory could not be achieved simply by relying on volunteers.

In January 1916 conscription was introduced and many more men from Nefyn, and indeed from right across Wales, were compulsorily drafted into the army despite considerable opposition from within the Welsh chapels. Those Nefyn men who felt that they had grounds for exemption from military service were forced to go before local tribunals. Although the folk in Nefyn knew little about the horrors of life in the trenches they did what they could to provide comforts and support for their men folk at the front.

But it was not only during the fighting on land that Nefyn men were exposed to danger. Before the war, Britain had depended to a great extent upon its merchant fleet. In 1914 more than two thirds of the food needed in these islands was imported, as well as vast amounts of raw materials for industry. Once the hostilities commenced it was up to the men of the merchant fleet to keep the sea routes open so that the home nations could be adequately supplied.

The captains of the large German U-boat fleet, armed with torpedoes and mines, were determined to stop supplies from getting through, and by the end of 1916 they were sinking about 300,000 tons of British shipping each month. In a maritime community like Nefyn the men who manned the merchant ships were bound to suffer heavily. Towards the end of the war, when it was feared that food supplies might run out, some rationing was introduced.

In the spring of 1918, as the war with Germany neared its end, an even more deadly enemy than the German military made its appearance. This was the Spanish 'flu pandemic which began to ravage the peoples of the world, including soldiers at the front. Unfortunately, even in a fairly remote place like Nefyn, the inhabitants were unable to escape its attentions.

The Early Days of the War
Initially, in places like Nefyn, life continued much the same as it had done before the war started. Some of the town's young men joined the army, left home and returned on leave to be seen marching along the street in their army uniforms. John Ifor Davies recounts how he and his friend, Robert 'Dolwen', were hugely impressed by the sight of David Williams, a tall well-built young Nefyn man who had recently joined the cavalry. He 'carried a leather stick and wore spurs which meant that he not only looked magnificent but also clinked sweetly as he walked.' One or two others temporarily left the Merchant Navy to join the Royal Navy, and they returned home in their smart naval uniforms. David Williams's brother, Ellis Hugh Williams, served in mine-sweepers as well as Q ships which were vessels bristling with guns although they had the appearance of merchant ships.

Because Britain had a fairly modest regular army at the outbreak of the hostilities, Lord Kitchener, the Secretary of State for War, embarked upon a massive recruitment campaign. Companies of soldiers visited towns and villages across the land to inspire young men to enlist. John Ifor Davies recalled that one day he paused outside the Old Nefyn Post Office, together with his younger brother, to watch a company of kilted Scottish soldiers, who were playing drums, fifes and bagpipes. They were parading up and down on Y Groes, their kilts swaying as they marched. At one point in the proceedings the sergeant-major in charge of the troop picked up John Ifor's little brother, Gwilym, and carried him up and down the line of soldiers. This, of course, was part of Kitchener's drive to recruit more volunteers. Incidentally, as a Royal Artillery officer during the Second World War, Gwilym subsequently distinguished himself in North Africa and Italy, as we shall see later.

On another occasion, as John Ifor was walking through Pwllheli with his grandmother he saw a tall man addressing a large crowd outside Salem chapel. This was The Revd John Williams, Brynsiencyn, who was drumming up support the war.

The People at Home in Nefyn
At home the people of Nefyn were remote from the war, and they continued with their daily lives as before. In December 1914 the *North Wales Chronicle* reported, 'The Madryn Hall was crowded last week when Sarn Dramatic Society performed a Welsh drama with very great credit.'[1]

Family members who remained at home knew little about what was happening at the front. Sometimes letters and cards would arrive in Nefyn, sent by sons and husbands who were on the Western Front but they gave no indication of the dreadful conditions their men folk were experiencing. When one Nefyn mother received letters from her soldier son she noticed that he had written 'Ypres' at the top of each letter. She was convinced that he was asking for money ('Y pres' in Welsh), for she had no idea that Ypres was a Belgian town which was the centre of much fierce fighting.

Folk tried to do what they could to support their Welsh soldiers serving in foreign parts. Relatives sent parcels to their men folk at the front and local groups were organised to provide comforts for soldiers. An article in the *North Wales Chronicle* in 1916 reported, 'In the Lleyn and Eifionydd division, the work of providing comforts for Welsh troops has been carried on with good results.... Nevin 33 pairs of socks, 19 mittens, 16 mufflers.'[2] The report goes on to state that Nefyn also provided pairs of gloves for the troops, but the actual number is not specified.

School children across Llŷn were involved in the war effort too. They were urged to scour the fields and grazing lands to collect sheep's wool from the hedges and bushes. The wool was then taken to school, from where it was despatched to the Government so that it could be sold to help pay for the war.[3]

The Nefyn Golf Club decided to close its links for the duration of the war. The *North Wales Chronicle* commented, 'They were of the opinion that the groundsmen could be more usefully employed on the land in other capacities. A large number of English visitors have become members of the club, several of whom are in the forces. The course will be reopened and put in playing condition after the declaration of peace.'[4]

As the war continued, people in Nefyn occasionally caught glimpses of sights which reminded them of the conflict. One afternoon a British destroyer steamed into the bay at Nefyn where it remained for several hours. A number of local boys, who were walking back to school after dinner, decided to head for the beach so that they could have a look at it. They were so impressed by the sight of the huge naval vessel as it lay at anchor that they spent too long staring at it. As a consequence they arrived at school late for afternoon lessons and were soundly admonished for their lack of punctuality.

On one occasion in 1916 German submarines were sighted off the northern coast of Llŷn, while in 1917 convoys of merchant ships were spotted making their way along the coast. Convoys were intended to minimise the risk to merchant shipping. By 1917 lone vessels had suffered such heavy losses at the hands of German U-boats that it was decided to band ships together in large numbers, protected by warships or armed merchant vessels. This device did help to reduce the loss of merchant shipping from about mid 1917 onwards.

After a time news began to reach Nefyn that young men from the parish had been killed in battle, or lost at sea, and every week local newspapers contained the details, and sometimes the photographs, of soldiers and mariners from North Wales who had been killed during the hostilities.

In the closing stages of the war food became scarce and, from January 1918 onwards, some rationing was introduced. Initially sugar was rationed, and in April 1918 meat, butter, cheese and margarine were added to the list. In an agricultural and fishing community like Nefyn food shortages were probably less acute than they were in most urban areas where, on occasions, people beccame so desperate for food that rioting almost broke out.

Conscription 1916

In 1916 conscription was introduced because the British army had suffered such heavy losses, and the number of men volunteering to join up had fallen. In January of that year single men aged 18-41 were compulsorily drafted into the army, and in the following year conscription was extended to include married men also. Before the war ended the age limit was raised to 51 years.

Nefyn men who were of military age and who wished to seek exemption had to appear before 'Lleyn Tribunals' which would then pronounce judgment on the merits of their cases. In 1916 a Nefyn dentist appealed on the grounds that he was the only dentist in northern Llŷn, and he was granted an exemption for one month.[5] In February 1917 Mr J. H. Jones of Nefyn was granted conditional exemption on the grounds that he had previously served for 12 years in the army (including service during the South African War) and since then he had broken his leg. An appeal was made by Captain William Williams of Nefyn on behalf of a motor bus driver, on the grounds that the company now had only two drivers instead of four. A decision on this case was deferred. Conditional exemption was granted to Robert Jones, Morfa Nefyn, but the appeal made by Robert Owen, Llwyn y Gwalch, was turned down.[6]

A firm condition of exemption was that men who had been excused military service had to attend weekly drill sessions in the Pwllheli Drill Hall, presumably to ensure that they had received some training in case their exemption expired or was subsequently overturned.

At a tribunal in March 1917 it emerged that several exempted Nefyn men had resolved not to attend the weekly drill sessions, and therefore it was decided to review their certificates of exemption. One such person was a Morfa Nefyn farmer, Evan Hughes, who had been granted exemption so that he could continue to assist his father on the family farm. When asked why he had refused to attend the drill sessions he replied, 'I do not wish to learn how to kill anyone.' When asked if he was prepared to join the drill sessions in future he replied, 'I shall not bear arms upon any consideration.' His exemption was promptly withdrawn.[7]

As the war progressed so many men were conscripted into the army that there was a shortage of suitable manpower on local farms. When agricultural workers were called up for military service the authorities agreed to provide substitute workers. However, this scheme did not meet with the approval of local farmers, several of whom said that they would prefer to share the services of farm workers rather than accept substitutes offered by the War Office.[8] Llŷn farmers also complained bitterly about the difficulty of securing the services of a blacksmith, for the majority had been conscripted to shoe the vast number of horses that were being used by the army during this war. It was also pointed out that the absence of rabbit catchers had resulted in the pests multipying to such an extent that they were seriously damaging valuable crops.[9]

The Revd J. Ellis Williams at the National Eisteddfod 1916

Despite the fighting, the National Eisteddfod was held as usual, apart from in 1914. The *North Wales Chronicle* reported in August 1916 that The Revd J. Ellis Williams, the winner of the chair at the recently-held National Eisteddfod at Aberystwyth, was a native of Nefyn. He had been in business with his brother, Mr O. M. Williams, before leaving to go to Bangor College. It states that 'he frequently competed at local eisteddfodau and it is known that he almost carried off the chair at one of the recent National Eisteddfodau.'[10]

The Sinking of *HMS Hampshire* 1916

In 1916 there occurred a disaster which shocked the people of these islands and which had a special significance for the inhabitants of Nefyn. On 5th June the armoured cruiser, *HMS Hampshire*, set out from her Orkney base at Scapa Flow to sail to the northern port of Archangel in Russia. On board, in addition to a large crew, was the Secretary of State for War, Lord Kitchener, who was on his way to visit Russia with his entourage of advisers. He was intending to meet the Russian Tsar to explain the Allied war policy and to discuss the provision of munitions.

Shortly after leaving port, *HMS Hampshire* ran into atrocious weather, and the captain decided to return to base. The cruiser was only about one and a half miles from the Scottish coast when she struck a mine, one of many that had recently been laid by a German U-boat. There was a deafening explosion amidships, and within 15 minutes the warship had disappeared beneath the waves, together with most of the personnel on board.

On hearing about the disaster, the Commander-in-Chief of the Grand Fleet despatched four destroyers and several patrol vessels to area, but by the time they reached the scene there was no trace of survivors and little evidence of wreckage. Fourteen men had managed to reach the shore on a ship's life raft, but two of them died as a result of their injuries before they could be given medical attention.

There were only 12 survivors from the sinking of the *Hampshire*, and over 600 men had perished including Lord Kitchener himself. The news of Kitchener's death stunned the British people, for he was considered integral to the war effort, as well as being a highly acclaimed military hero after his victory at the Battle of Omdurman in the Sudan in 1898.

However, it was news of another person's death which saddened the people of Nefyn most of all. A young Royal Naval Reserve officer from the town, Lieutenant Evan Hughes Williams Tŷ Canol who was the son of Captain William and Mary Williams, had also lost his life when the *Hampshire* went down. His name appears on the Nefyn War Memorial together with the names of all the other sailors and soldiers who lost their lives during the Great War.

At that time few people knew that it had been the intention of Lloyd George, Minister of Munitions and Nefyn's Member of Parliament, to accompany Kitchener on that fateful Russian visit. Because the Easter Rising had recently erupted in Ireland, Prime Minister Herbert Asquith had asked Lloyd George to remain behind in London. History is full of questions which begin with the words 'What would have happened if . . . ?' Invariably such questions are impossible to answer but, if Lloyd George (later to become Prime Minister and inspirational wartime leader) had gone down with Kitchener on *HMS Hampshire*, one thing is certain – the course of history in Nefyn, Caernarfonshire, Wales, Ireland and the whole of Britain would have been very different!

Three Fatal Wartime Accidents in Nefyn

Not every tragedy that occurred in Nefyn at this time could be attributed to the war. One Friday evening in October 1916 an omnibus belonging to the 'Nevin Motor Omnibus Company' met with a serious accident as it travelled between Pwllheli and Nefyn, resulting in the death of one person and serious injuries to several others.

A local newspaper recorded the details of the incident.[11] It was an extremely dark night, and the rain was particularly heavy, as the 'bus made its way along the road past Boduan. On board were several Nefyn children who were returning home for the weekend from Pwllheli County School, for they had to lodge in the town during the week. Also on the bus were a number of adults including Alderman G. Hughes Roberts from Edern and Mrs Davies, the wife of Mr Ellis Davies MP. The driver was Thomas Jones, Y Fron, Nefyn.

When the 'bus reached the crest of Boduan Hill the driver stopped to allow a passenger to get off. Suddenly the 'bus began to roll backwards. Alderman Hughes Roberts leapt from the vehicle so that he could place some stones behind one of the wheels, but he was unable to stop the vehicle. The 'bus continued to run backwards down the hill, gathering speed alarmingly the further it travelled. Finally it crashed into a stone wall at the bottom of the hill, turned a complete somersault and came to rest upside down. The driver of the 'bus was killed instantly, several of the children and one or two of the adults were injured, and it took nearly two hours to release everyone from the upturned vehicle.

At the Nefyn inquest into the 'bus driver's death a verdict of 'Accidental Death' was recorded, but the coroner concluded that the cause of the accident remained a mystery. The omnibus appeared to be in good working order, and witnesses confirmed that Thomas Jones was a competent driver and mechanic. An inspection of the 'bus had revealed that the gears had not been engaged, and neither of the two brakes had been applied. Therefore it was suggested that the driver must have released the handbrake before attempting to engage the gears, thus causing the 'bus to roll backwards down the steep hill at a great speed. The jury recommended that in future all omnibuses should be equipped with wheel blocks and iron drop bars at the rear in order to prevent them from rolling backwards out of control. A vote of sympathy was passed to the driver's widow and her five children.

The second fatal accident involved a quarry worker. Quarrying was a particularly hazardous occupation, and the local newspapers carry numerous reports of deaths among the employees in the North Wales slate and granite quarries. On 22nd May, 1918, 63 year old Mr Richard Roberts,

Cae Glas, Mynydd Nefyn, was drilling rock at a Caernarfonshire County Council quarry on Garn Boduan when a large quantity of stone and soil fell on top of him. He fell, broke both his legs and suffered serious head injuries from which he subsequently died. Once again a verdict of 'Accidental Death' was recorded.

Another fatal road accident occurred on Friday 9th August 1918, but this time it involved a pony and trap. Mr Daniel Jones, Terfyn Morfa Nefyn, had taken a Morfa resident and her aged mother to Llithfaen. On the return journey, as the trap was descending a steep hill, a rabbit ran across the road in front of the pony, which immediately bolted. As the driver struggled to control his pony the harness suddenly snapped and the trap ran free. It hurtled down the hill, collided with an embankment and overturned, trapping the two ladies beneath it. Mrs Catherine Griffiths of Siop Rhandir, Morfa Nefyn, suffered severe head injuries from which she died two days later. Her daughter, Mrs Thomas, sustained a fractured arm and head injuries. At the inquest on Mrs Griffiths a verdict of 'Accidental Death' was recorded, and the coroner expressed the opinion the Mr Daniel Jones had done all that he could to avoid the accident.[12]

The Sinking of the *SS Dora*, 1917
The *SS Dora*, owned by the Liverpool-based 'Aberdovey and Barmouth Steamship Company', was the little coaster which kept the communities of northern Llŷn supplied with goods during the years leading up to the Great War. She was purchased by the company in 1900 to replace the previous vessel, *SS Telephone*, and she became a much loved sight in the area.

The *Dora* sailed every Friday from Liverpool to Porth Dinllaen, Aberdovey and Barmouth, carrying groceries and other essential supplies, as well as a few passengers. At Porth Dinllaen she would tie up beside the specially-built warehouse, known locally as 'Warws Dora'. Here she would unload some of her cargo which would be distributed to shopkeepers, farmers and builders in various parts of the peninsula.

One of *Dora*'s most experienced and long-serving masters was Captain David Williams of Morfa Nefyn, who had previously served on sailing ships. His father-in-law, Captain Robert Jones, was the company's agent at Porth Dinllaen. *Dora* made her last visit to Porth Dinllaen in October 1915, after which she was transferred to the Liverpool to Belfast crossing on the instructions of the War Office.

On 1st May 1917, about 11 miles from the Scottish coast, the *Dora* was intercepted by a German U-boat. Captain Williams and his crew were ordered to take to the lifeboats and, as soon as the little ship had been evacuated, she was torpedoed and sunk. News of the loss of the *Dora* was greeted with much sadness right across Llŷn. Following the destruction of their ship, the captain and his crew were left to fend for themselves, but they eventually came ashore on the Mull of Galloway, the southern-most point in Scotland. Afterwards Captain Williams went on to skipper other vessels, including the *Wheatcrop* in 1927.

Following the destruction of the *Dora*, the 'Aberdovey and Barmouth Steamship Company' was wound up. The havoc caused by German U-boats during the war and the high cost of a replacement vessel had damaged the confidence of those running the company.

Bodies Washed up on the Northern Coast of Llŷn 1918
In 1918 several bodies were washed up on the northern coast of Llŷn, including that of a tall, slim, middle-aged man which came ashore between Nefyn and Pistyll. These grisly occurrences were the aftermath of a double maritime tragedy which occurred in the Irish Sea – the accidental loss of the *SS Burutu* on 3rd October 1918 and the sinking of the *RMS Leinster* by a German U-boat a week later on 10th October.

The *SS Burutu* was a 3863 ton merchant ship belonging to the Elder Dempster Company, and for many years she had traded between Liverpool and the west coast of Africa. Recently she had been attacked off the coast of Liberia by a German U-boat which she had managed to fend off, since she was defensively armed. However, during this engagement two crew members had been killed and the ship had been so badly damaged that she was forced to put into port for repairs before continuing her journey. Eventually, as she headed towards Liverpool in dense fog, she collided in the Irish Sea with another merchant vessel, the *City of Calcutta*, which was on her outward journey. The *Burutu* sank straight away, and 148 crew members and passengers lost their lives.

A week later, on the morning of 10th October *RMS Leinster*, a mailboat belonging to the City of Dublin Steam Packet Company, set out from Kingstown (now Dun Laoghaire) bound for Holyhead. On board were 771 persons, including 77 crew members, 22 Dublin Post Office workers, 180 civilian passengers, 489 military personnel and three Royal Navy gunners who were manning the 12 pound guns.

The *Leinster* had been at sea for about an hour when she was attacked by a German U-boat which fired three torpedoes at her. The first missile missed, the second struck the sorting room, killing all but one of the Post Office workers, and the third smashed into the engine room. Immediately the ship began to sink, and by the time rescue boats arrived only 271 people could be saved. The 500 who lost their lives included Welsh, Irish, Scottish, English, Canadians, Americans, New Zealanders and Australians. The sinking of the *Leinster* was the worst maritime tragedy ever to occur in the Irish Sea.

In due course several bodies from the *Burutu* and the *Leinster* were washed up along the northern coast of Llŷn, including the body of the middle-aged man which came ashore near Nefyn.

War-time Visitors to Nefyn
Despite the hostilities, visitors continued to come to Nefyn each summer. In the summer of 1918 it was reported, 'in spite of the war conditions visitors are flocking in hundreds from the Midlands and London. Every town from Aberystwyth to Pwllheli, Nefyn and Aberdaron is crowded with visitors.'[13] It was also reported in 1918 that there would be sufficient food for all visitors arriving at Cricieth, Porthmadog, Pwllheli and Nefyn but, 'on account of the rationing, they must either arrange a transfer from their own food office or obtain an emergency ticket at the resort where they are temporarily residing"'.[14]

The Death of Sergeant McCurdy 1918
In August 1918, three months before the end of the war, news reached Morfa Nefyn that Sergeant John Nevin McCurdy had lost his life in a drowning accident in France. For many years John McCurdy, who had been born in Ireland, had been in charge of the telegraph/telephone office in Morfa Nefyn. He was an extremely popular person who 'took a practical interest in all affairs affecting the general welfare of the community.'[15] For several years he had been Treasurer of the Nefyn Golf Glub.

During the war John McCurdy joined a signal company of the Royal Engineers and was sent to France as a telegraph/telephone operator. Tragedy struck in the closing stages of the war when he decided to go swimming in the sea at Le Havre. Some distance from the shore he developed cramp and was forced to call for help. Two local youths swam to his assistance, but they soon became exhausted. Realising that if he continued to cling on to them all three would drown, Sergeant McCurdy released his grip and sank. News of the death of this popular person was received with great sadness, especially in Morfa Nefyn.

His funeral at Le Havre was a spectacular affair, described thus in the *North Wales Chronicle*, dated 23rd August, 1918:

> The coffin was followed by a detachment of military and an army chaplain. Then came the British soldiers carrying 12 beautiful wreaths

in British and French national colours, the colours of Le Havre and also of the signal service. Around the tomb, during the prayers, respectfully stood officers and 100 British soldiers, a delegation attached to the signal service and representatives of the French telegraphs and telephones as well as a small group of French friends.

Sergeant McCurdy's name does not appear on the Morfa Nefyn War Memorial but it is recorded on the North Wales Memorial Arch in Bangor and his details are posted on the Commonwealth War Graves Commission site:

> John Nevin McCurdy   Cairn Nevis   aged 51   Sergeant   "L" Signal Company Royal Engineers   Service No. 27329   Date of Death 10/08/1918   Husband of Lizzie McCurdy of Morfa Nefyn.   Buried Ste Marie Cemetery, Le Havre

The Cessation of Hostilities 1918

On 15th November 1918 the *Caernarfon and Denbigh Herald* reported, 'Shortly after 11 o' clock on Monday morning (11th November, 1918) the welcome news of the cessation of hostilities reached Pwllheli. This news was announced to the country by the firing of rockets, which was heard at the far end of the peninsula.'

Obviously there was an enormous sense of relief that the war was finally over, although the parish does not seem to have staged the same sort of joyous celebrations which subsequently marked the end of the Second World War. It was reported that the people of Nefyn held a thanksgiving service, during which the vicar, The Revd R. C. Jones, expressed the thanks of the people of the parish to the Prime Minister (Lloyd George) for the prominent part he had played in securing the peace.[16]

The Influenza Pandemic of 1918-19

The Great War had resulted in the deaths of millions of people, but before the guns had fallen silent there struck a killer virus which proved to be far more costly in terms of human life than the war itself. It was a virulent outbreak of influenza, commonly known as the Spanish 'flu, and it was responsible for the deaths of an estimated 50 million people across the globe, including soldiers from both sides in the Great War. The pandemic started in March 1918 and it lasted until June 1919.

If a person caught the 'flu it usually turned very quickly to pneumonia with fatal results. It was a condition which affected not only babies, children, the sick and the elderly but also strong healthy young men and women. In

November 1918 the *Caernarfon and Denbigh Herald* reported, 'The epidemic is very severe in the rural districts. At Nevin five deaths took place in one family. Mrs Kate Jones, Cefn y Maes, and her baby died in the same week. She was only 26.'[17] Having been discharged from the army, owing to severe war wounds, 22 year old John Owen Jones, Cefn y Maes, contracted the illness and within days he had died of pneumonia. He had been married for only five weeks. His wife's sister also succumbed to the disease and her mother was reported to be seriously ill too.[18] Among other local victims of the influenza outbreak were the wife and only son of Mr Owen Williams, the Head of Nefyn Council School.

Nefyn and Morfa Nefyn Sailors during the Great War

Many Nefyn and Morfa men performed vital roles in the Merchant Navy during the Great War. Not only did they keep Britain supplied with food and essential raw materials, they also transported soldiers and munitions to the front. Captain Henry Parry, Caerau, carried troops in *SS Lake Michigan*, *RMS Grampian* and *RMS Metagama*, all of which had been commandeered for war service. Between August 1914 and January 1916 he transported 37,000 troops, including British, Australian and Indian soldiers as well as the men of the Canadian Expeditionary Force. He carried them to ports in France, Egypt, Gallipoli and Salonika. Captain Richard Griffith, Llysarborth, was carrying munitions to the Middle East when his ship *SS Samantha* was torpedoed and sunk near Alexandria.

At first some U-boat commanders would order the crew of a British vessel to abandon ship before sinking it, but later on most enemy captains adopted a policy of torpedoing vessels on sight without any warning. Altogether 24 sailors from the parish lost their lives during this conflict, and most of them were killed when their ships were torpedoed by German U-boats during the period from June 1916 to the end of 1917.

There were many Nefyn seamen who, despite experiencing the sinking of their ships, survived to sail again. One such person was Evan Davies, Hafan, Morfa Nefyn, who was torpedoed twice during the hostilities. This was the same Evan Davies who, as a teenager, had survived the earthquake in Sicily in 1905. He was 3rd Officer on the *SS Diplomat* when his ship was sunk by the German raider *Emden* in the Bay of Bengal. When he was torpedoed for a second time in the Irish Sea by a German U-boat, he and the other ship's officers managed to save their vessel by beaching it, an action for which they were rewarded by the admiralty.

Captain Henry Owen, Dolwen, was also torpedoed twice. He was master of the *SS Llandudno* which was sunk in August 1917 and the *SS Clarissa*

Radcliffe which was torpedoed in March 1918. Despite his experiences he continued in service until 1929.

Other Nefyn mariners who escaped after their ships had been sunk included Captain Griffith Jones (the *Grenada* – sunk by a U-boat 1916; Captain Evan Davies, Cartra, (the *Delphic* which was a war loss 1917); Captain William Davies (*Belford* –sunk 1917); Captain Hugh Roberts (*Jane Radcliffe* – sunk 1917); Captain John Williams (*Lowmount* – war loss 1917); Thomas R. Wilson (*Jane Radcliffe* – sunk 1917); John Jones (*Hylas* – torpedoed 1917); Captain Hugh Jones (*Boltonhall* –torpedoed 1918); Captain G. Owen (*Uskmoor* – torpedoed 1918).

Some Nefyn sailors were officially recognised for their services and acts of courage during the war. Captain John Williams Min-y-Mor was mentioned in despatches and handsomely rewarded for his actions which resulted in the destruction of two German warships. When his sailing ship, the *Conway Castle*, was attacked by the German light cruiser Dresden, the crew members were taken prisoner and the *Conway Castle* was sunk. Some time later, when the *Dresden* began to run short of food, her captain decided to land all his prisoners at Valparaiso in order to conserve rations. Now that he was ashore, Captain Williams immediately notified the Admiralty of the exact longitude and latitude in which his ship had been sunk, and he was able to provide vital information about both the *Dresden* and her sister ship, the *Emden*. As a result of his actions the *Emden* was quickly hunted down and destroyed by the Australian cruiser, *Sydney*, while the British cruisers *Kent*, *Glasgow* and *Orana* located the *Dresden* and put her out of action. Some time later, after the war had finished, Captain Williams was invited to London where he was presented with a cheque for £1000.[19]

As a young sailor, Rowland Davies (later to become Captain Rowland Davies, Fernlea, master of the *Thistleford* during World War II) was awarded the Lloyd's Silver Medal for Gallantry; Robert David Owen OBE, Bay View, was decorated for skilfully avoiding the attentions of a German U-boat; Daniel Evans, later to become a captain for the Elder Dempster Company, was awarded the Distinguished Service Cross for war service in August 1917; and Captain John Groth was commended for his war service in November 1917.

The two parish war memorials record the names of the following sailors from Nefyn and Morfa Nefyn who perished during the hostilities:

Hugh Davies Pen y Craig   aged 18   Third Mate on *MV Arabis* (London)   Lost 16/09/1917   Son of Evan and the late Janet Davies of Nefyn
Thomas G. Davies   Fron Cottage   aged 30   Second Mate on *SS Exford* (Cardiff)   Lost 14/07/1917   Son of Jane Davies and the late Robert Davies of Nefyn

Humphrey Griffith Tŷ Newydd aged 37 Carpenter on *SS Llandudno* (London) Lost 01/08/1917 Son of Ann Griffith and the late William Griffith. Husband of Catherine Griffith of Nefyn

Richard Griffith Llysarborth aged 37 Master of *SS Semantha* Lost 14/10/1917 Husband of Mary Griffith of Nefyn

William Griffith Bodwyn aged 51 First Mate on *SS Edernian* (Cardiff) Lost 20/08/1917 Son of the late Hugh and Alice Griffith Husband of Ann Griffith of Nefyn

Hugh Griffith Hughes Bryn Glas aged 17 Ordinary Seaman on *SS Edernian* (Cardiff) Lost 20/08/1917 Son of Seth and Eliza Hughes of Nefyn

Richard Hughes Plas aged 35 Donkeyman on *SS North Wales* (London) Lost 24/10/1916 Husband of Margaret Hughes of Stryd y Plas, Nefyn

Evan Jones Bryn Beuno aged 59 Master of a ship which was sunk due to enemy action Lost 23/5/1917 Husband of Ellen Jones

James Jones Bodfan aged 43 Fireman on *SS Broomhill* (Newcastle) Lost 10/05/1917 Son of Ellen and Robert Jones Husband of Ellen Jones of Morfa Nefyn

Robert Jones Castle aged 37 Fireman on *SS Broomhil*l (Newcastle) Lost 10/5/1917 Son of Robert and Ellen Jones Husband of Margaret Ellen Jones of Nefyn

Robert W. Jones Fron Terrace aged 31 Bosun on *SS North Wales* (London) Lost 24/10/1917 Son of Daniel Jones Husband of the late Kate Jones of Nefyn

Edwin Lloyd Tai Lôn aged 17 Ordinary Seaman on *SS Cymrian* (London) Lost 25/08/1917 Son of Jane Lloyd and the late John Lloyd of Nefyn

Evan H. Owen Sunnyside aged about 37 Lost at sea due to enemy action Son of Elizabeth and Rhys Owen of Morfa Nefyn.

Griffith Owen Erw Goch aged 45 Master of *HMT North Wales* Lost 24/10/1916 Son of the late Captain Henry and Catherine Owen Husband of Jane Owen of Morfa Nefyn

Hugh David Owen Isfryn aged 23 Seaman on *SS Canganian* (Cardiff) Lost 20/08/1917 Son of Griffith and Margaret Owen of Morfa Nefyn

James Owen Oakfield aged 44 Master of *SS Beacon Light* (Liverpool) Lost 19/02/1918 Son of the late James and Jane Owen, Morfa Nefyn

William James Owen Oakfield aged 40 Carpenter on board *SS Beacon Light* (Liverpool) Lost 10/02/1918 Son of late James and Jane Owen, Morfa Nefyn Husband of Grace Alice Owen

William Roberts Cae Rhyg aged 15 Ordinary Seaman on *SS Cymrian* (London) Lost 25/08/1917 Son of John Jones Roberts and Catherine Roberts of Nefyn

Henry Thomas   Gwylfa   aged 19   Able Seaman on *SS Lorle* (West Hartlepool) Lost 11/06/1918 Son of Richard and Maggie Thomas, Stryd Fawr, Nefyn

Hugh Thomas Sea View aged 19 Carpenter on *SS Canganian* (Cardiff) Lost 17/11/1917 Son of Jane Thomas and the late William Thomas, Morfa Nefyn

William Thomas Sea View aged 50 Bosun on *SS Canganian* (Cardiff) Lost 17/11/1917 Husband of Jane Thomas, Morfa Nefyn

Robert Thomas Bwlch Glas aged 48 Bosun on *SS Camelia* (North Shields) Lost 27/11/1917 Son of the late William and Gwen Rees Thomas

Evan H. Williams Tŷ Canol aged 30 Lieutenant Royal Naval Reserve *HMS Hampshire* Lost 05/06/1916 Son of Captain William and Mary Williams of Nefyn

William Williams   Glan Morfa   aged 26   Carpenter on *SS North Wales* (London) Lost 24/10/1916 Son of William Williams and the late Mary Williams of Morfa Nefyn

Nefyn and Morfa Nefyn Soldiers during the Great War
Many men from the parish served in the army between 1914 and 1918. They took part in the campaigns in Flanders, France, Gallipoli, Palestine and Mesopotamia. Some received awards for service and gallantry like Richard Davies, Bryn Cytun, Morfa Nefyn who was awarded the Medal of King Albert I of the Belgians for service on the Belgian front.

Several others, like Private J. H. Ensor, the son of Mr George Ensor, Stryd y Plas, were wounded in action. Apparently, during the fighting in France, he came under ferocious attack. A piece of shrapnel from a shell cut off the toes on his left foot and a bullet passed through his right foot.[20] Despatch rider Robert Williams, the son of Mr & Mrs Thomas Williams of Stryd y Plas, was more fortunate. He had a lucky escape when a huge fragment of shrapnel struck his motor cycle and completely destroyed it. The rider escaped with a minor wound to his leg.[21] Another Nefyn man, David William Davies Liverpool House, suffered 38 bullet wounds and lost an arm at the Battle of Ypres.[22]

Often the conditions in the trenches on the Western Front were almost intolerable, and sometimes soldiers suffered gravely, even during lulls in the fighting. One such person was Private John Hughes, Stryd y Llan, who was taken to a military hospital suffering from severe frostbite.[23] Others, like J. T. Williams Tyn'rardd, David Griffiths Fron Oleu, R. J. Jones (who later became the Nefyn chemist) and Tom Nefyn Williams (who took part in the ill-fated Gallipoli campaign) all returned home with wounds from which they never fully recovered. While some soldiers came back from the trenches with physical wounds, many more returned with mental scars which would remain with them for the rest of their lives.

Altogether the names of twenty-one young soldiers from NetFind and Morfa who died during this conflict are recorded on the two war memorials in the parish. They are:

William Griffith   Pool Street   Born Nefyn   Enlisted at Nefyn   Private   1st/6th Battalion Royal Welch Fusiliers   Service No. 1606   Died of wounds received in action in France 24/02/1915   Buried Morfa Nefyn Churchyard

Griffith Hughes   Cefn y Maes   Killed in action during the Great War   No further details known

Morris Hughes   Buarth   aged 31   Private   4th Battalion Royal Welsh Fusiliers   Service No. 203968   Died of wounds received in action 31/03/1917   Son of Robert and Mary Hughes, Morfa Nefyn   Buried Morfa Nefyn Churchyard

Evan W. Jones   Old Post Office   aged 30   Corporal   55th Machine Gun Corps   Service No. 35540   Killed in action in France 14/04/1918   Son of William and Ellen Jones of Nefyn   Buried Le Plantin Graveyard, France

John Jones   Pen y Bryn   aged 36   Private   'K' Company Army Service Corps   Service No. 216817   Died in Aldershot Military Hospital from wounds received in action 17/10/1916   Son of Richard and Sydney Jones of Morfa Nefyn   Buried in Morfa Nefyn Churchyard

John O. Jones   Cefn y Maes   aged 22   Private   47th Battalion Royal Welsh Fusiliers   Service No. 3274   Died of pneumonia and wounds received in action 12/11/1918   Husband of Mary Jones   Buried in Morfa Nefyn Churchyard

Thomas Jones   Caer Berllan   Enlisted at Cricieth   aged 30   2nd Battalion Royal Welch Fusiliers   Service No. 266595   Killed in action in France 01/10/1917   Son of David and Ellen Jones of Nefyn   Buried in Le Grand Hasard Military Cemetery, Morbecque.

Edward J. Owen   Noddwyn   aged 21   Enlisted at Caernarfon   Private   10th Battalion Royal Welch Fusiliers   Service No. 26184   Killed in action in France 20/07/1916   Son of the late Mr & Mrs Owen Owen of Penrhos, Morfa Nefyn; grandson of Mrs Ellen James and The Revd Edward James of Morfa Nefyn   Recorded on the Thiepval Memorial

Evan M. Owen   Glanaber   aged 21   Born Ceidio   Enlisted at Bangor   Corporal   14th Battalion Royal Welch Fusiliers   Service No. 20901   Killed in action in France 10/04/1916   Son of William and Margaret Owen, Morfa Nefyn   Buried Bethune Town Cemetery

George Owen Tŷ Llewelyn   Enlisted Caernarfon   aged 23   Private   1st/6th Battallion Royal Welch Fusiliers   Service No. 3264   Killed in action in the Gallipoli campaign 03/09/1915   Husband of Mary Owen of Nefyn   Recorded on the Helles Memorial

William Owen   Dyffryn   aged 19   Private   1st Battalion South Wales Borderers   Service No. 46864   Killed in action in France 18/04/1918   Son of Owen and Ann Owen of Morfa Nefyn   Recorded on the Loos Memorial

Evan Roberts   Cae Glas   Born Nefyn   aged 39   Enlisted Wrexham   Private 1st Battalion Royal Welch Fusiliers   Service No. 5348   Killed in action in France 16/05/1915   Son of Richard Roberts and the late Elizabeth Roberts of Mynydd Nefyn   Recorded on Le Touret Memorial

Evan O. Roberts   Tyddyn Ffynnon   aged 24   Enlisted Liverpool   Private 1st Battalion Royal Welch Fusiliers   Service No. 40327   Killed in action in France   03/09/1916   Son of Robert and Margaret Roberts of Nefyn   Recorded on the Thiepval Memorial

John T. Roberts   Ddor Ddu   aged 19   Private   58th Training Reserve   Service No. 48724   Died of wounds received in action 28/03/1917   Son of David and Janet Roberts   Buried in Nefyn New Cemetery

Richard Roberts   Tanymaes   aged 32   Private   15th Battalion Lancashire Fusiliers   Service No. 25643   Killed in action in Flanders 10/07/1917   Son of Robert and Margaret Roberts of Tyddyn Ffynnon   Husband of Gwen Roberts of Nefyn   Buried in Coxyde Military Cemetery, Belgium

John G. Thomas   Fron Terrace   aged 20   Enlisted Bangor   Private   17th Battalion Royal Welch Fusiliers   Service No. 203778   Killed in action in France 29/10/1918   Son of Mr J. & Mrs E. Thomas of 3 Fron Terrace Nefyn   Buried in Awoingt British Cemetery, France

William G. Thomas   Gwylfa   aged 21   Private   10th Battalion Sherwood Foresters   Service No. 74213   Died in Bermondsey Military Hospital (London) from wounds received in action in France 07/11/1918   Son of Richard and Margaret Thomas of Nefyn   Buried in Nefyn New Cemetery

Evan Williams   Penrallt   Born Nefyn   aged 40   Enlisted Mold   Private   10th Battalion Royal Welch Fusiliers   Service No. 37608   Killed in action in France 18/08/1916   Recorded on the Thiepval Memorial

Griffith Williams   Glan Fadryn   Enlisted Caernarfon   aged 18   Private 1st/6th Battalion Royal Welch Fusiliers   Service No. 3273   Killed in action at Gallipoli 06/11/1915   Son of William and Mary Williams of Morfa Nefyn   Recorded on the Helles Memorial

John A. Williams   Glan Ogwen   aged 38   Enlisted Caernarfon   Private 1st/6th Battalions Royal Welch Fusiliers   Service No. 266181   Killed in action in Palestine 06/11/1917   Son of John and Jane Williams   Husband of Mary Jane Williams of the Tower, Nefyn   Buried in Beersheba War Cemetery

John G. Williams   Bodawen   aged 30   Killed in action in France 18/10/1918   Son of the late John and Jane Williams Bryn Glas, Nefyn   Memorial inscription in Nefyn New Cemetery

Notes
1. *NWC* 28/12/1914
2. *NWC* 00/00/1916
3. *NWC* 10/05/1918
4. *NWC* 05/01/1917
5. *C&DH* 10/03/1916
6. *NCW* 09/02/1917 & 16/02/1917
7. *NLW* 23/03/1917
8. *NWC* 09/03/1917
9. *NCW* 26/10/1917
10. *NWC* 25/08/1916
11. *NWC* 13/10/16
12. *C&DH* 16/08/1918
13. *NCW* 02/08/1918
14. *NCW* 15/02/1918
15. *NCW* 23/08/1918
16. *C&DH* 29/11/1918
17. *C&DH* 23/11/1918
18. *C&DH* 15/11/1918
19. *C&DH* 18/09/1925
20. *NCW* 29/09/1916
21. *NCW* 29/09/1916
22. mentioned during the 'Tân yn Llŷn' court case at Caernarfon Assizes in 1936
23. *NWC* 22/02/1918

Chapter 4

The Inter-War Years 1919-1939

Introduction

The end of the Great War was greeted with a huge sense of relief, but many local families had suffered so much in such a short time. It is true that, for many decades, sea-faring families in Nefyn and Morfa Nefyn had lived constantly with the fear that they might lose loved ones, and indeed drowning at sea was a fate which a great many mariners from the parish had suffered over the years. But the loss of life during the Great War was a totally different matter. Within a relatively short time 46 men from Nefyn and Morfa Nefyn had lost their lives, not as a result of unavoidable natural disasters but because they had been killed by enemy action.

Some Nefyn families had been hit particularly hard. Robert and Margaret Roberts lost two sons on the Western Front in 1916-17; Robert and Ellen Jones had lost two sons when the *SS Broomhill* was torpedoed in May 1917; Jane Thomas, Sea View, Morfa Nefyn, had lost both her husband and her son when the *SS Canganian* was sunk in November 1917; Richard and Margaret Thomas, Gwylfa, had lost two sons aged 19 and 21 within the space of five months in 1918; Jane Owen, Oakfield, Lôn Uchaf, Morfa Nefyn, lost two sons, James and William, when the *SS Beacon Light* was torpedoed in February 1918.

The terrible loss of life incurred during the conflict remained firmly in many people's minds. As in almost every village and town across Wales, the inhabitants of both Nefyn and Morfa Nefyn were determined not to forget their young men who had lost their lives. During the early 1920s war memorials were erected by both communities, and a new village institute was built in Morfa Nefyn. This was to be a recreational facility for everyone in the village but especially for the young people. All this was achieved by means of public subscription.

The effect of the war generally upon Welsh life had been devastating across the nation. Before the war there had been a certain Liberal optimism in the country; the number of Welsh speakers had been high; the Welsh chapels had been buoyant; and there were plenty of employment opportunities locally, not only at sea but also in the quarries and on the farms.

After 1918 the people were war weary, and many were grieving for lost family members; communities across the land had lost a generation of their

Welsh-speaking youth, including many of their most talented young men; Welsh Liberalism had become disaffected on account of conscription and the horrors of the war, both of which did not sit easily with the values preached by the chapels; agriculture, which had been boosted during the war, now fell into depression; sett production had almost ceased in the Nefyn quarries, for granite setts had given way to tar macadam for road building; and the crippling post-war trade recession virtually brought to an end the great Nefyn seafaring tradition which had seen generations of young men follow their fathers, uncles and grandfathers to sea. All this resulted in a period of hardship and austerity. To men returning home from the front, their country did not seem like 'a land fit for heroes', as Lloyd George had promised.

During the war sailing vessels had proved to be particularly vulnerable to U-boat attack, and by this time they had virtually had their day. However, after 1918 a few Nefyn captains and sailors, like Captain William Davies of the *Monkbarns*, kept faith with the old sailing barques and fully-rigged ships. Despite the difficulties caused by the economic recession of the 1920s, there were still some young Nefyn men whose preferred option was a career at sea, although most of them were now serving on steamships. Several men from the parish went on to serve in the Merchant Navy throughout the inter-war years and into the Second World War.

Towards the end of their careers a few Nefyn and Morfa master mariners served as shore superintendents for the larger shipping companies. For example, Captain Owen Bay View, became a Shore Superintendent for the Blue Funnel Line; Captain John Lloyd Moorings, occupied a similar position in Rio de Janeiro; and Captain Dan Evans Tynllys, served in New York as Marine Superintendent for the Elder Dempster Company from 1923-1933.

In February 1926, Porth Dinllaen received its first motor lifeboat named MOYE, which had been on show at the British Empire Exhibition at Wembley in 1925. To accommodate this new vessel the slipway and the boathouse had to be modified at a cost of £10,000.[1]

After the war motor omnibuses ran more and more services to and from Nefyn. In 1922 Garwen Hughes, a Nefyn hairdresser, set up the Blue Bus Company with a depot in Stryd y Llan. There were now three 'bus companies running regular services between Pwllheli, Nefyn, Morfa Nefyn and Edern – the Cambrian Railway Company, the Nefyn and District Omnibus Company and the Blue Bus Company. Needless to say, there was frantic competition between the rival companies for passengers and quick journey times. By the outbreak of the Second World War all three of the local 'bus companies had been absorbed into the larger Crossville Company.

Despite the introduction of motor omnibuses, during the summer months visitors to Nefyn could enjoy a nostalgic link with the past when an old horse-drawn stagecoach, complete with postilion blowing his horn and a driver cracking his long whip, would arrive outside the new Nanhoron Arms, carrying visitors who had recently arrived at Pwllheli railway station.

It was during the inter-war years that the private motor car and motor cycle became more popular, although few Nefyn people owned any form of motorised transport. A car was considered a luxury, reserved for a few of the most affluent members of the community. However, as early as 1917 there was a motor garage in Morfa Nefyn where W. P. Roberts overhauled and repaired cars and sold motor accessories. During the late 1920s there were two motor engineers within the parish – Claremont Garage, Morfa Nefyn, and T. J. Hughes in Stryd y Llan, Nefyn. By 1936 O. H. Parry had opened the Red Garage in Nefyn which advertised new and second-hand cars and motor cycles for sale, motor accessories and repairs, as well as British cars for hire. E. Roberts, Stryd y Ffynnon, also advertised cars for hire.

Car hire advertisements at this time were clearly aimed at holiday-makers to the area, for between the wars Nefyn was attracting a greater number of summer visitors. A 1922 guide book[2] describes Nefyn as a clean and healthy fishing town with beautiful sand, safe and pleasant bathing, a mild but bracing climate, magnificent scenery, pleasant cliff walks and an unlimited supply of pure water. People who were wealthy enough to take a summer break would arrive either in their own cars or by omnibus from Pwllheli railway station. They came mainly from Lancashire, Cheshire and the Midlands. They stayed in local hotels, they rented apartments and houses or they were accommodated in the numerous guest houses within the parish.

In the *North Wales Business Directory* for 1933, in addition to the Nanhoron Arms and the Sportsman, there were three private hotels listed for the parish – Caeau Capel in Nefyn and the Cecil and the Tremydon in Morfa Nefyn. A large new hotel, 'The Linksway' was built in Morfa Nefyn in 1936. Many Nefyn and Morfa families took paying guests into their homes during the holiday season. John Jones Tawelfa owned a couple of boats which he hired out to summer visitors, and there were several young Nefyn men who were always eager to take paying customers for a boat trip around the bay. Clearly local people were gearing up to the burgeoning tourist trade.

An important improvement to the amenities in Nefyn and Morfa arrived in about 1928 when an electricity supply was brought to the area from the quarry at Carreg y Llam where it was used to power the crushing machines which processed the lumps of granite into aggregates and railway ballast. For most people the paraffin lamp now gave way to the electric light bulb.

However, not every household was connected to the electricity supply immediately, and a few families, especially those living on Mynydd Nefyn, were still using paraffin lamps during the Second World War.

In places like Nefyn much of the religious, cultural and social life in the communities still revolved around the chapels. The Sabbath was considered a day of rest, and attendance at chapel (often twice each Sunday) was still the norm for many Nefyn families. In addition, many people attended a variety of chapel meetings, societies and functions during the week.

The Nefyn Council School remained an all age school, catering for children from five years of age until they reached the school leaving age. Those children who passed the scholarship examination went to Pwllheli County School (known as 'Town School') and from Monday to Friday they had to lodge in the town, coming back to Nefyn for the weekends. Some Nefyn parents preferred to send their children to the residential schools in Towyn, Dolgellau or Bangor. Henry Parry, later to become the school dentist, attended the Towyn School while Gwilym Davies, John Ifor's younger brother, was a pupil at the Friar's School in Bangor.

Two major highlights of the Nefyn calendar each year continued to be the Easter Monday Nefyn Agricultural Show and the Summer Regatta and Sports, both of which were taking place before the beginning of the 20th century, as we have already noted. Apart from the Mownti at Easter and the Nefyn Regatta in August there was a full round of concerts, plays, singing festivals and eisteddfodau.

In the late 1920s and early 1930s film shows became popular. These silent films from America were shown in the Madryn Hall by Mr Greenwood, an Englishman, who accompanied the 'on-screen action' with appropriate sound effects which he played on a piano. On a Friday evening people would flock to the Madryn Hall to watch those flickering films, featuring such Hollywood stars as Charlie Chaplin, Mary Pickford and Douglas Fairbanks. The film shows were discontinued in the 1930s when talking films became fashionable.

Owing to the post-war depression, some Welsh-speaking folk in certain parts of rural Wales migrated to England to find work, while many Welsh people began to believe that they had more to gain by speaking English rather than Welsh. Throughout Wales, English was the language used for official purposes and many people considered it to be the language of social progress too. In terms of people's everyday lives, Llŷn remained steadfastly Welsh-speaking, although in places like Nefyn and Morfa Nefyn it must be remembered that large numbers of English-speaking visitors came to the area during the summer holiday season.

Across the nation fears for the future of the Welsh language were growing, but there was one person who was prepared to do something about it – Sir Ifan ab Owen Edwards. In 1922, following in the footsteps of his educationalist father, he founded a non-political Welsh-language youth organisation called Urdd Gobaith Cymru (*The Welsh Language of Youth*). For a few years prior to the Second World War, an Urdd camp was established in a field at Porth Dinllaen each summer.

In 1925, when the National Eisteddfod was being held at Pwllheli, a group of Welsh Nationalists met at a temperance inn on Y Maes. At this meeting Blaid Genedlaethol Cymru (*The Welsh Nationalist Party*) was formed. This upsurge in Welsh nationalism manifested itself dramatically in 1936 when members of the Welsh Nationalist Party symbolically set fire to some RAF installations which were under construction at Penyberth, Penrhos, a few miles from Nefyn. Three highly respected Welsh intellectuals handed themselves in and were arrested. Controversially, a Nefyn night watchman was one of the main witnesses at their trials.

The rise to power of the Fascist regimes of Hitler in Germany and Mussolini in Italy during the 1930s, and the danger posed by their territorial ambitions and mighty war machines, caused increasing alarm to the Westminster Government. Military installations, like the local airfields at RAF Penrhos (1936) and RAF Hell's Mouth (1937), were constructed to meet the danger, and it would not be long before Europe would be plunged into war again. This time, as never before, everyone would be required to play their part – those who sailed the seas, those who fought on land, those who took to the air, and the entire civilian population on the Home Front.

The *North Anglia* Tragedy 1922
Three years after the end of the Great War, with its horrendous loss of life, the folk of Nefyn had to face yet another tragedy. The deaths of four Nefyn seamen on the *SS North Anglia* would once again cast a huge dark shadow over the entire town.

The *SS North Anglia* belonged to the fleet of Hugh Roberts, a former Edern schooner captain who had moved to Newcastle to establish a shipping company in partnership with Edward Beck. Called Hugh Roberts & Company of Newcastle, the firm switched from sailing vessels to steamers and it was renamed 'The North Shipping Company'. Because Hugh Roberts was so closely connected with Llŷn, many of the company's captains, seamen and investors also came from the peninsula.

In April 1922 the 3562 ton steamer *North Anglia* left Falmouth in ballast bound for Rio de Janeiro, and on Good Friday she ran into a ferocious storm

The coastguard lookout at Penrhyn Porth Dinllaen

A bunker at RAF Nefyn, the wartime radar station

Porth Dinllaen

One of the tees at the Nefyn Golf Club at Porth Dinllaen

Evidence of a landslide in the cliffs at Nefyn

Cors Geirch, a local area of wetland which is a Site of Special Scientific Interest

Warws Dora to which coasters brought supplies from Liverpool each week

The barren side of Garn Boduan which was ravaged by fire in 1979

A late 19th century postcard view of Y Groes and Stryd Fawr, Nefyn

The new sign, with a portrait of Cynan, at the Bryncynan Inn

The Caeau Capel Hotel in Nefyn where Clement Attlee sometimes stayed

The former coastguard cottages at Morfa Nefyn

MILWYN

WILLIAM GRIFFITH	POOL STREET
GRIFFITH HUGHES	CEFN-Y-MAES
EVAN W. JONES	OLD POST OFFICE
JOHN O. JONES	CEFN-Y-MAES
THOMAS JONES	CAER BERLLAN
EVAN M. OWEN	GLANABER
GEORGE OWEN	TY LLEWELYN
EVAN ROBERTS	CAEGLAS
EVAN O. ROBERTS	TYDDYN FFYNON
JOHN T. ROBERTS	DOOR DOU
RICHARD ROBERTS	TAN-Y-MAES
JOHN G. THOMAS	VRON TERRACE
WILLIAM G. THOMAS	GWYLFA
JOHN A. WILLIAMS	GLANOGWEN

The names of Nefyn soldiers who died in the Great War

1939 — 1945

OWEN ROBYNS-OWEN, GWYNLE
ELISEUS GRIFFITH JONES, ANGORFA
WILLIAM WILLIAMS, PRIMROSE VILLE
THOMAS IDRIS JONES, TALYLLYN
EDWIN GRIFFITH WILLIAMS, GLAN MORFA
OWEN EMRYS WILLIAMS, CAE BACH
REES GWYN OWEN, SUNNYSIDE

The names of Morfa Nefyn men who died in the 1939-45 war

The Morfa Nefyn War Memorial

The Nefyn War Memorial

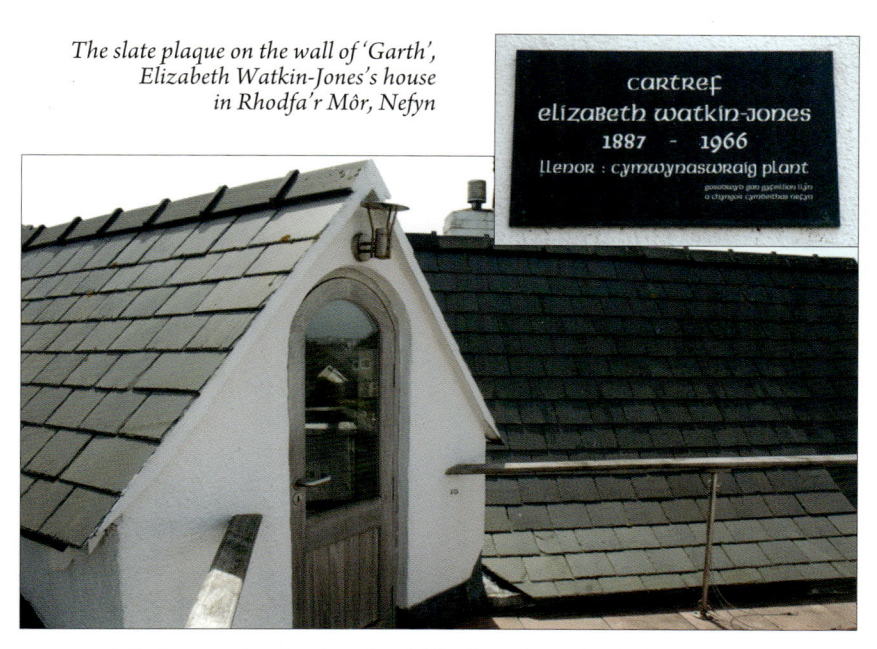

The slate plaque on the wall of 'Garth', Elizabeth Watkin-Jones's house in Rhodfa'r Môr, Nefyn

The balcony at Garth where the children's author, Elizabeth Watkin-Jones used to take a break from her writing

The Hetty Rampton on the slipway at Porth Dinllaen

The new Canolfan at Nefyn, built in 2010

A sign in Nefyn to commemorate the twinning of the town with Porth Madryn in Patagonia

A stone tablet in Porth Madryn (inscribed in Welsh) to commemorate the twinning

in the Bay of Biscay. As she hit mountainous seas some of her hatches flew open, dangerous gear was hurled around the deck and the vessel almost capsized. It is not clear what caused the ship to become unstable. Some folk maintained that the ballast was incorrectly stowed; others hinted that the hatches were not securely battened down, allowing water to get into the holds; there were also rumours that heavy equipment had been left lying loose on the deck. Whatever the reason, the consequences were disastrous.

Two Nefyn seamen, Moses Jones Penpalment, and John Williams Arvonia, were lost overboard. Two others, Richard Jones (the brother of Moses) and Daniel Henry Jones Fron Terrace were fatally injured. Another Nefyn man, Robert Williams Mona View who was one of the ship's officers, was hurled through an open hatch into the hold. He sustained a dislocated shoulder, a fractured skull, and a torn scalp which 'hung down over his eyes like a curtain' – injuries which caused him to remain in a coma for several days. Other members of the crew received a variety of less serious injuries.

Owing to the deaths and injuries amongst the crew, the steamer returned to Falmouth so that the casualties could be transferred to hospital. The bodies of Richard Jones and Daniel Henry Jones were transported to Pwllheli and, on the day of their funerals, their coffins were carried by horse-drawn hearse to the Bryncynan Inn. Almost the entire population of the town turned out for the funeral and all business was suspended. At the Bryncynan the funeral cortege was met by an enormous crowd of Nefyn men who walked the last mile in a long procession behind the coffins.

When the cortege reached the Nefyn Public Cemetery the coffins were carried to the graveside by local sailors. At the committal ceremony a telegram from Captain Helm, master of the *North Anglia*, was read out. He conveyed his condolences to the two families concerned, and added that "the Welsh sailors had faced the terrible ordeal of the storm bravely and with magnificent heroism."[3]

The ship's officer, Robert Williams, never fully recovered the use of his arm, and the visible damage to his head was a constant a reminder of the terrifying ordeal that he and the rest of the crew had faced that day. Despite his horrific injuries he continued with his career at sea for another twelve years.

The Nefyn and Morfa Nefyn War Memorials 1923

In 1923 the Nefyn and Morfa Nefyn War Memorials, which had been paid for by public subscription, were unveiled to the memory of those local men who had lost their lives in the Great War. The Morfa Nefyn memorial is situated inside the churchyard of Sant Mair, while the Nefyn memorial stands on a refuge in the middle of the road which leads to Morfa Nefyn, near its junction with Rhodfa'r Môr.

In 1922 the *North Wales Chronicle* reported that a heated discussion had taken place within the town concerning the proposed Nefyn War Memorial.[4] A War Memorial Committee, under the chairmanship of Captain J. D. Griffiths, had been given the task of making all the necessary arrangements. News leaked out that the committee was intending to erect the memorial without including the names of the Nefyn men who had lost their lives. This provoked a public outcry, and in March 1922 a meeting was convened to discuss the matter.

At that meeting Captain Griffiths reiterated the committee's decision not to have any names inscribed on the memorial. The overriding feeling of the meeting was that the names of those who had lost their lives should be recorded. Relatives who had lost loved ones during the conflict, as well as the ex-servicemen present, felt particularly strongly about this matter. Amid rapturous applause Captain Williams declared that, if the names were not included, the memorial would be pulled down!

Mr Owen Williams, a member of the War Memorial Committee, stated that he could understand people's feelings, but he insisted that there was the question of finance, as well as other considerations. Captain Williams replied that, if necessary, he would find the additional money within 48 hours. This response was greeted with another round of deafening applause.

Mr Thomas Jones (Chairman of the Parish Council) asked if the present meeting was legal because seven days notice had not been given. Mr J. Davies, an ex-soldier, yelled, 'Did the Germans give us seven days' notice?' Once again there was thunderous applause.

Dr Shelton Jones, Pwllheli, (President of the local branch of the Comrades of the Great War) and Councillor T. J. Williams both expressed the opinion that the views of the ex-servicemen and the relatives of the war dead ought to be respected.

In the end the protesters won the day, and the Nefyn War Memorial, complete with the names of local soldiers and sailors who had been killed, was finally unveiled at a ceremony on Friday February 23rd 1923. From a historian's point of view, it is just as well that the vocal majority succeeded in getting their way, for a war memorial which does not record the names of those who died is of no value whatsoever as an enduring record.

Jane Jones, Tŷ Coch Inn, Porth Dinllaen

Mrs Jane Jones was a remarkable lady who became famous throughout Llŷn as the harbourmaster at Porth Dinllaen and the innkeeper at the Tŷ Coch Inn, where she also ran a private school for the children of mariners.

Jane Jones was baptised Jane Ellen Thomas in Caernarfon in about 1836. In the summer of 1856 she married Thomas Irvin Linton at Caernarfon, and a daughter, Jane Eliza Linton, was born in Liverpool. In the autumn of 1866 Thomas Linton died at Liverpool aged 43. By that time there were four children aged eight, seven, five and three years.

In the autumn of 1868 she married Hugh Humphrey Hughes at Caernarfon, and shortly afterwards the family moved to Llŷn, where in due course they took up residence in the Tŷ Coch Inn. At this time the hamlet of Porth Dinllaen was a sizeable and thriving community and, according to the 1861 census, there were 72 people living in the dwellings on the beach. Unfortunately, shortly after settling into Tŷ Coch, Jane's second husband died at the age of 42. By this time there was a fifth child aged one year and Jane was expecting another baby.

In 1881 she married Captain William Jones, a Nefyn-born master mariner, and they had a son, also named William. Mrs Jones continued to run the Tŷ Coch Inn where she provided refreshment for local workers and visiting mariners. Her school, where she taught children reading, simple arithmetic and needlework, is mentioned in Slater's Directory of 1880. Some Nefyn children, like Mary Hughes from the shop at Nanhoron House, were educated at Jane Jones's school. It was probably still operating in 1901 when her son William Jones was recorded as a pupil-teacher.

In the 1920s Mrs Jones achieved notoriety as the only woman harbourmaster in the British Isles. Her responsibilities involved ensuring that the regulations of Porth Dinllaen harbour were adhered to, so that it was a safe place for both boats and sailors. Her duties were not very onerous, for at that time the importance of Porth Dinllaen as a port was greatly diminished. Few ships came into the bay, apart from steamers like the *Rebecca* which brought shop goods, and the steamers, *Tyfan* and the *Maggie Purvis*, which delivered cargoes of coal onto the beach. Consequently her rewards as harbourmaster were correspondingly meagre. Her remuneration consisted of a copy of each *Shipping Gazette* which she displayed in the Tŷ Coch Inn so that local people could follow the movements of ships.

Mrs Jane Jones died on December 3rd 1933 at the ripe old age of 97 years, and she is buried in Saint Edern's churchyard alongside her third husband.

The Final Attempt to Extend the Railway to Nefyn 1924
We have already seen that, mainly due to lack of finance, all previous attempts to construct a railway line to the northern coast of Llŷn had been

abandoned before the outbreak of the Great War. However, in 1924 the Great Western Railway Company drew up plans to extend the line from Pwllheli to both Nefyn and Abersoch. Clearly the company's intention was to carry holiday-makers by train to the two most important Llŷn holiday resorts not yet accessible by rail, for the nearest line ended at Pwllheli. Furthermore, a railway line which reached the northern coast of Llŷn, and which stretched down the peninsula as far as Abersoch, would have benefited local farmers, whose produce could be transported more quickly by rail to centres of population.

Detailed plans were drawn up, arrangements were made for the compulsory purchase of land and a Parliamentary Bill was passed. On leaving Pwllheli the line to Nefyn would follow the present Ala Road, before crossing the river and the road to Abersoch. It would proceed behind Bodegroes Park and the village of Efailnewydd, after which it would run parallel to the main Pwllheli-Nefyn road before turning northwards in a huge arc close to Glan y Gors. Finally it would cross the Nefyn road and skirt around the foot of Garn Boduan before terminating at a station at the bottom of Stryd y Plas.[5]

In August 1925 it was reported that the GWR scheme to extend the railway line to Nefyn and Abersoch had 'for the present been abandoned on financial grounds.'[6] It appears that the finance to carry out these extensions failed to materialise in the future too, for the railway lines to Nefyn and Abersoch were never constructed.

The Revd John Owen Williams at Nefyn

The Revd John Owen Williams, Congregational minister, poet and Archdruid of Wales from 1928-1934, resided in Nefyn from time to time during the 1920s.

He was born on 21st May 1853 at Gatehouse, Madryn, a short distance from Nefyn. Both his parents died when he was very young, and so he was brought up by his Aunt Jane in Llanbedrog. As a child he received no formal education outside the Sunday School, and he entered the world of work at the age of 12. At first he was employed as a gardener before moving to Liverpool in his early twenties to work for a provisions merchant. In that city he joined the Welsh Wesleyan Chapel and became a local preacher. In 1881 he joined the Kensington Congregational Church in Liverpool, and soon afterwards he was invited to become its pastor. He was ordained in 1884, and he remained the minister of that church until his retirement in 1930. In 1927 he became chairman of the Union of Welsh Independents.

John Owen Williams was a well-known and highly successful participant at the National Eisteddfod of Wales, and he assumed the bardic name Pedrog after the 6th century Celtic saint who established his llan at Llanbedrog where The Revd Williams had grown up. He won the chair four times – Porthmadog in 1887, Swansea in 1891, Llanelly in 1895, and Liverpool in 1900 – and he also won the gold medal. For many years he was an adjudicator at the National, and he contributed many articles and poems to Welsh newspapers and periodicals. He was also the poetry editor of several Welsh publications. In 1917 he was awarded an honorary MA degree by the University of Wales – not a bad record of achievement for someone who never had the opportunity to go to school!

In 1928, as Archdruid Pedrog of Wales, he had the honour of conducting the ceremony which marked the revival of the ancient 'Gorseth Kernow' (*the Gorsedd of Cornwall*). During the 1920s Pedrog was a frequent visitor to Plevna in Rhodfa'r Môr, the Nefyn home of Captain Evan and Mrs Davies who had been members of his congregation in Liverpool. John Ifor Davies recalls going to Capel Soar as a child when Pedrog was preaching. Apparently he was a tall erect man with a neatly trimmed white beard and 'the look of a dignified benevolent patriarch.' He had a reputation for having a great sense of theatre when he was preaching, so that his congregation would be sitting on the edge of their seats. Pedrog died in Liverpool on 9th July 1932.

Nefyn Fishermen and the Marauding Seals 1925

It was reported in January 1925 that large colonies of common and grey seals, which were breeding in the remote Llŷn inlets, were stealing fish from the fishermen's nets in Nefyn Bay, causing a great deal of damage. On one occasion it was estimated that they had taken several hundred fish from the nets and in doing so had torn the mesh to shreds. As a consequence, the fishermen of Nefyn had been forced to spend an entire week mending their nets instead of catching fish and earning a living.

The Ministry of Agriculture and Fisheries was alerted and the naval gunboat *HMS Doon* was despatched to the area, where it managed to shoot three of the animals. But still the creatures refused to be scared away. At about the same time Lord Wavertree, the well-known Liverpool racehorse owner and Jockey Club member, was staying at the Nanhoron Arms Hotel so that he could play golf on the Nefyn course. He heard about the seal problem, and one day when he was on the golf course he noticed several of the animals, basking on the rocks. Immediately he abandoned his round of golf, and sent someone to fetch a heavy rifle. That morning he killed eight of the creatures and a Captain Kneeshaw from Abergele shot another two.[7]

Despite such efforts, the seals continued to pose problems for local fishermen. Several years later in December 1933, it was reported that Nefyn fishermen had once again suffered 'a considerable loss' when swarming hungry seals seriously damaged a large number of valuable nets.[8]

The Solar Eclipse of 1927

Wednesday 29th June 1927 was the day on which, in certain parts of Wales and England, people would have the opportunity to see a rare total eclipse of the sun. It was stressed that this event would not be witnessed again in Wales until the year 2151. The eclipse was due to hit Llŷn first before proceeding north eastwards over Snowdonia, the Conwy area, Lancashire and North Yorkshire. The event had been widely publicised in the press, and crowds of people travelled to North Wales to witness this amazing phenomenon.

On the day of the event the railway companies ran special trains from London, Birmingham, Manchester and Liverpool, arriving at Pwllheli station between 5.00 am and 5.30 am. All the hotels and boarding houses in Nefyn and the other resorts in the region were fully booked, and in the early hours of that Wednesday morning local inhabitants and visitors alike climbed hills and mountains in the area so that they might obtain the best possible view. People gathered on Yr Eifl, Mynydd Nefyn, Garn Boduan, and Garn Fadryn. Others massed on the sea front at Pwllheli while many clambered to the top of Snowdon.

Unfortunately for the waiting crowds, the weather that morning was not conducive to viewing solar events. Everywhere was covered by low cloud and a damp mist; there was a biting wind and the rain poured down incessantly so that everyone became thoroughly drenched. And as for the solar eclipse – the spectacle was totally obscured by the mist and the heavy rain clouds. Consequently the waiting crowds did not even catch a glimpse of that amazing spectacle. The *Caernarfon and Denbigh Herald* sums up the occasion thus: 'The eclipse in North Wales, and especially in Caernarvonshire, was a fiasco, rain and clouds in the majority of places blotting out the spectacle from the view of many thousands of visitors.'[9]

A Ship Beached at Porth Dinllaen 1927

People walking along the beach at Porth Dinllaen towards the end of October 1927 would have seen the strange sight of a large steamer stranded on the sand.

On October 23rd 1927 the Hull coaster, *SS Matje*, and another vessel were battling their way along the Llŷn coast in a storm force gale. The captains of both ships decided to send out distress signals which were soon spotted on land, and the Porth Dinllaen lifeboat was alerted. However, the wind was so strong that the lifeboat coxswain and the secretary had to crawl along the headland on their hands and knees for fear that they would be blown over the edge.

When they reached the boathouse the tide was so high and the waves were so strong that the sea was washing inside, and some of the rollers had been wrenched from the slipway. Under the circumstances it was considered impossible to launch the lifeboat, and so it was delayed until the tide had ebbed. Neither the *Matje* nor the other vessel was in any immediate danger, since they were drifting away from the rocky coast. The lifeboat was launched at midnight and, since both vessels seemed to coping, she simply stood by. At 2.00 am the weather improved slightly, and both ships managed to make their way to the relative safety of the bay, but the *Matje* had lost both her anchors. Concerned that his vessel could not be secured, the captain decided to run the *Matje* full steam ahead onto the beach. This he managed to do, but it was not until five o'clock the next morning that the lifeboat was able to return to the safety of the harbour wall. When daylight arrived and the tide had gone out, the black-hulled steamer could be seen lying lopsided on the sand like a huge stranded whale.

A Nefyn Sea Captain's Gallantry Award 1929

In 1929 Captain Evan Davies of Cartra, Rhodfa'r Môr, was master of the White Star liner *RMS Baltic*. From 1917 he had been master of a string of White Star vessels including *Athenic*, *Crelic*, *Canopic*, *Vedic*, *Tropic*, *Gallic*, *Haverford*, *Delphic*, *Persic*, *Regina* as well as *Baltic*. Evan Davies was the son of Hugh Davies, the nailer from Stryd y Llan, who had taught many aspiring young Nefyn seamen the rudiments of navigation.

On 6th December 1929, having set out from New York in a severe storm to return to Liverpool, *RMS Baltic* came across the Newfoundland schooner, *Northern Light* which was sailing from St John's to Bonavista Bay. She was flying a distress signal.

Very skilfully, Captain Davies managed to manoeuvre the huge White Star liner to a position windward of the schooner and then he despatched a lifeboat to rescue the schooner's crew of five.

Subsequently Captain Davies was awarded the Lloyd's Silver Medal for saving life at sea. He was also presented with a medal and a sum of money by the Life-Saving Benevolent Association of New York for a notable act of heroism at sea during a violent storm; and he was given a testimonial on vellum by the Government of Newfoundland. The *Baltic*'s 3rd Officer and nine crew members were also rewarded for their actions during that rescue.

The Porth Dinllaen Coastguard Station Established about 1930
As early as 1880 there had been a coastguard in these parts. His name was Thomas John Thomas and he operated along the northern coast of Llŷn from Nefyn to Aberdaron. His duties involved patrolling the coastline, visiting wrecks, and writing reports about things which he observed during his travels.[10]

In about 1930 a permanent coastguard look-out was established on the headland at Porth Dinllaen, and several cottages were built near the golf course to house the coastguards and their families. Although the station closed many years ago, the small stone-built look-out post can still be seen on the point, and the former coastguard dwellings are now used as holiday cottages. In April 1939 one of the coastguards, 53 year old James Henry Mclaughlin, was fatally injured when he attempted to jump from a moving Crossville bus as it approached crossroads adjacent to the Linksway Hotel.[11]

Today the Coastguard Service at Porth Dinllaen consists of a team of eleven volunteer rescue officers who are available to respond to emergencies at any time of the day or night. Because of the nature of the northern coastline of Llŷn, members of the team are fully trained in cliff rescue procedures. Their work can involve searching for missing persons, rescuing people trapped on the cliff face and descending the cliffs to reach people stranded on inaccessible stretches of the shoreline. Based at the Porth Dinllaen Coastguard Rescue Station, the team has at its disposal a four wheel drive vehicle which is equipped with a wide range of rescue and safety equipment. They often work in conjunction with the local lifeboat and the Search and Rescue helicopters from RAF Valley.

A more recent initiative has been the National Coastwatch Institution which was established in Britain in 1994. It is a charity operated entirely by volunteers who maintain a visual watch along Britain's busy coasts and who monitor the radio channels when visibility is poor. Therefore they are the 'eyes and ears along the coast'. Coastwatch personnel are trained in chart and map reading as well as in dealing with emergencies.

In 2007 National Coastwatch acquired the Porth Dinllaen lookout post and, with financial assistance from 'The Big Lottery Fund', they transformed it into an operational base once again. The Porth Dinllaen lookout post became fully operational in April 2010. At first the post was manned only at weekends and bank holidays only, but at present Coastwatch volunteers are on duty every day of the year apart from Christmas Day.

The Revd Tom Nefyn Williams
The Revd Tom Nefyn Williams was a Calvinistic Methodist/Presbyterian minister and evangelist who became extremely well-known in Llŷn, and indeed throughout Wales.

Born in 1895 at Bronolau, Boduan, he was the son of John Thomas Williams and his wife Ann. John Thomas was a small time farmer, poet, musician and lay preacher. The family moved from Boduan into the neighbouring parish where they established themselves at Bodeilias, a smallholding facing the sea on the side of Mynydd Gwylwyr. It was here that Tom and his brothers grew up.

When Tom left Nefyn School at the age of 13 he went to work in the Eifl Granite Quarry while his two brothers chose careers at sea. Following the outbreak of war in 1914 Tom joined the army, serving in France, Gallipoli, Egypt and Palestine. His army war service changed his life, for the hardship and the horror he experienced made a lasting impression on him. After the war he returned to Nefyn, a committed pacifist. He produced a pamphlet denouncing war, and he also published a booklet entitled, 'At Suvla Bay: What a soldier learnt at Gallipoli'. It told of his dreadful experiences during the disastrous Gallipoli campaign.

After the war he was so determined to preach the gospel of peace to his fellow men that he became an itinerant preacher, holding services not only in local chapels but also on Y Groes, on the beach and on the cliff top. J. Ifor Davies records how, as children, he and his friends would follow Tom Nefyn to Capel Pisgah on Mynydd Nefyn, where so many people had gathered to hear him preach that the crowds were spilling out through the doorway.

Tom Nefyn was eventually persuaded to put himself forward for the full-time ministry, and so he enrolled at the Porth Bible School in the Rhondda, before continuing his theological studies at the Calvinistic Colleges in Aberystwyth and Bala. These two colleges were well-known for their modernistic approaches to theology. Tom was ordained in 1925, married his wife, Ceridwen Roberts, and received a call to the pastorate at Ebenezer Chapel, Tumble, on the edge of the South Wales Coalfield where there was a considerable amount of political and social unrest. This was the era of the 1926 General Strike in Britain.

It was during his ministry at Tumble that Tom Nefyn came into conflict with the Presbyterian authorities, for Tom Nefyn regularly delivered his social and political views from the pulpit. He preached passionately against the social injustice which he saw around him – low wages, poverty and the disgraceful state of coalminers' houses. He was determined to take care of his flock's physical needs as well as their spiritual well-being. His ideas about the nature of the church and his modernistic doctrinal views also caused great consternation within the South Carmarthenshire Presbytery and the South Wales Association which viewed them as bordering on heresy. On the other hand, he gained tremendous respect and popularity among the members of his congregation and within the local community. In fact, Tom Nefyn's ministry at Tumble brought many people back into the church.

His differences with the Presbyterian hierarchy dragged on for several years, and matters came to a head when he was asked to renounce his views or resign. After a time he decided to offer his resignation, but the Ebenezer congregation refused to accept it. In 1928, much to the alarm of his congregation, he was suspended from the ministry. The Ebenezer flock continued to support their former pastor, but the local Presbytery decided to dissolve the church at Tumble and lock the doors of the chapel building. The members of the Ebenezer congregation were informed that they were no longer members of the Presbyterian Church.

The Tumble congregation then decided to purchase a plot of land so that they could build their own place of worship. They assumed that Tom Nefyn would continue to be their pastor, but he had returned to Llŷn. Subsequently he spent a period of time in a Birmingham Quaker retreat, after which he made his peace with the Welsh Presbyterian authorities and sought reinstatement as one of their ministers. His former Tumble chapel members were distraught.

During the rest of his ministry The Revd Tom Nefyn Williams served in a number of churches in North Wales including Gerlan, Pwllheli and Edern in Caernarfonshire. During the remainder of his life he continued with his evangelistic style of ministry, leading worship not only in the chapels but also in village halls, in clubs, in public houses and on street corners. He became a familiar figure in Nefyn, conducting open air services on Y Groes or on the beach where he would preach, play his portable harmonium and lead the assembled people with his lusty singing.

One November evening in 1958, after conducting a service in the chapel at Rhydyclafdy, he collapsed suddenly and died. A memorial stone outside the chapel commemorates his passing, and a plaque on the wall of the Bethania chapel in Pistyll is dedicated to his memory. To some Welsh people The Revd Tom Nefyn Williams remains a controversial character who 'rocked the Welsh Presbyterian boat', but in his native Llŷn many folk remember his life and work with tremendous affection.

The Rescue of Two Sea Planes at Porth Dinllaen 1933
The strange sight of two seaplanes stranded on the beach at Porth Dinllaen, one of them badly damaged and lying at an awkward angle on top of a beach hut, must have attracted many sightseers in February 1933.

On February 24th two Supermarine Spitfire flying boats had set off from Stranraer in Scotland bound for Calshot, their base at the edge of Southampton Water. When they reached North Wales they ran into a snow storm and gale force winds. As they crossed Caernarfon Bay, so dangerous were the conditions that they were compelled to find shelter. They eventually dropped down into the bay at Porth Dinllaen, but the weather continued to deteriorate.

The next morning Porth Dinllaen coastguards noticed flares being fired into the air, and at 10.00 am it was established that they had come from the two flying boats, one of which had been damaged by the force of the waves. The lifeboat did not set out immediately because the tide was very high and the waves were crashing against the door of the boathouse. At 10.45 am the lifeboat was launched. With the lifeboat standing by, both seaplanes managed to make their way into Porth Dinllaen harbour.

But even the harbour could not afford a safe haven. As the storm intensified it was feared that the moorings of both aircraft would snap, and the two craft would be swept out to sea again. Therefore it was decided to beach both 'planes. Despite gale force winds and driving snow, both aircraft were successfully beached with the assistance of the lifeboat crew. But so fierce was the gale that both seaplanes were damaged in the operation, one of them eventually coming to rest on top of a beach hut.

John Glyn Davies
A frequent visitor to the Nefyn area during the inter-war years was John Glyn Davies, scholar, poet and writer of sea songs for children. He had strong ties with Llŷn, especially with Porth Dinllaen and Edern, where he used to stay.

John Glyn Davies was born in October 1870 in Sefton Park (Liverpool) where his father was a tea merchant and a prominent member of the Welsh community in the city. In 1887 he began work as a Liverpool shipping clerk. In 1899 he was prompted to begin work on creating a Welsh library at the University College of Wales, Aberystwyth, an undertaking which would later form the basis of the National Library of Wales. In 1907 he joined the staff of the library at the University of Liverpool, and subsequently became a member of the university's Celtic Department. Eventually he became Head of that department, a position that he held until his retirement in 1936.

Throughout his life he retained an intense interest in sailing ships and all things maritime, including the building of model ships for his son, a collection of which is now in the National Museum of Wales. When on vacation from his work at Liverpool University he would often come to Llŷn, travelling on the small cargo steamers which called in at Porth Dinllaen and staying at the mill in Edern.

In his poetry he wrote lovingly and evocatively about Llŷn, but he is best remembered for his series of children's songs which became familiar to generations of Welsh children – *Cerddi Huw Puw* (1923), *Cerddi Robin Goch* (1935) and *Cerddi Portinllaen* (1936). The songs of Huw Puw were based upon a real-life Liverpool mariner called Hugh Pugh, and his small vessel, the flat *Ann*. The songs which John Glyn Davies wrote were inspired by sailors' sea shanties he had heard as a young man when he worked as a clerk in the shipping offices at Liverpool Docks. Here is his own account of how he was first introduced to sea shanties:

> The arrival of the *Queen of Cambria* in the Mersey in 1893 gave me my first live interest in shanties. She was anchored in the Slyne, and I went off on the tug with Captain Henry Thomas who was to take her into Albert Dock at 2.00 am. It was a brilliant moonlit night, and I stood with the captain on the poop, watching the men weighing anchor. They sang a-roving......and to me it was the finest of all the sea shanties. Captain Thomas was an excellent singer with a great stack of songs, and during the time the ship was in dock I picked up many sea shanties from him.[12]

Many other shanties he acquired from his brother, Captain Frank Davies, who had sailed on the *Cambrian Queen* as an ordinary seaman. John Glyn Davies died at Llanfairfechan on 11th November, 1953 aged 83.

A Nefyn Night Watchman and The Great Fire of 1936
Worried by the growth of German militarism during the 1930s, the British Government decided to build additional military installations and airfields, including an RAF bombing school. Initially, potential sites for the bombing school were identified in Northumberland and Dorset, but they were abandoned in the face of local opposition. Subsequently the Air Ministry located the site at Penyberth, Penrhos, a few miles from Nefyn. Penyberth was one of the most historic homesteads in Llŷn, and there was an outcry amongst the people of Wales that this cherished old building was about to be destroyed so that a bombing school could be built there. Unlike the campaigns in England, the Welsh protests went unheeded. By September

1936 the ancient building had been torn down, and the work of constructing the RAF bombing school had commenced.

Just one week after Penyberth had been demolished, a great fire occurred on the site. In the middle of the night six wooden offices and workshops belonging to the Air Ministry, together with a huge store of timber, were set on fire. The flames, towering high into the sky, lit up the entire countryside. Throughout Wales it became known as 'Tân yn Llŷn' (*The Fire in Llŷn*). The total cost of the damage that night was estimated to be £2,671, a very considerable sum of money in those days.

Three highly respected Welsh intellectuals, Saunders Lewis (a university lecturer), The Revd Lewis Valentine (a Baptist minister) and D. J. Williams (a grammar school teacher) immediately went to the police station in Pwllheli, where they confessed to this symbolic act of arson. They were duly arrested and charged. Subsequently they appeared before Pwllheli magistrates and at the Caernarfon Assizes.

One of the main witnesses at these trials was the Penyberth nightwatchman, a Nefyn man who had lost an arm during the Great War. In 1917 he had fallen foul of the law whilst home on leave from the army. Together with an accomplice he had been sentenced by Pwllheli magistrates to three months imprisonment with hard labour for stealing two quarters of mutton, the property of Mr John Roberts, butcher.[13]

The Nefyn nightwatchman, who had been employed by the firm of Glasgow builders to guard the Penyberth site during the hours of darkness, now discovered that he was one of the main witnesses in the case against the three arsonists. At the Pwllheli and Caernarfon trials he gave evidence, under oath, that he had begun his duties at 5.30 pm. There had been a slight shower of rain when he had made his usual routine inspection of the site, accompanied by his lurcher dog. At 1.30 in the morning, as he was carrying out another inspection in total darkness, he alleged that he was suddenly grabbed from behind by two men who threw him to the ground. He stated that initially he thought somebody was having 'a bit of fun with him', but he soon realised that it was no joke. He told the court that he tried to call out to his dog which had run away, but was prevented from doing so by one of the men who placed a hand over his mouth. He maintained that he struggled to free himself from his captors, but his efforts were in vain since he had only one arm. He also stated that, as he lay on the ground, he was aware that a fire had been started nearby.

He reported that, some time later, the two men jumped up and ran away in different directions. It was at this point that he said he noticed fires burning all around, for the flames had been fanned by a strong north-westerly wind. On seeing the burning buildings, he claimed that he went to fetch a bucket of water, but by that time the fires were blazing in several different places about 20 or 30 yards apart. Eventually he ran to a nearby bungalow to raise the alarm. It was clear that his evidence was not compatible with the version of events provided by the three accused men who maintained that they had not seen anyone at the Penyberth site during that night.

At the Caernarfon trial the nightwatchman added to the evidence which he had provided at the Pwllheli hearing. He now stated that he was sure he had also seen two other men in the light of the fires, making a total of four altogether, but he was not able to recognise any of them.[14] The fact that the nightwatchman's evidence was at variance with the testimonies of the accused, together with the inconsistencies in his evidence at the two trials, did not go unnoticed. Counsel for the Prosecution suggested to him, 'I put it to you that you were not attacked by any man on that night', to which he replied, 'Well, I ought to know!'

During his summing up at the Caernarfon trial the judge stated that the jury might wish to discount the nightwatchman's testimony altogether, for he reminded the jury members that they were not required to make a decision as to whether or not there had been an assault that night. The three men in the dock, he pointed out, had been accused of arson, a charge to which they had confessed. However, at the conclusion of their deliberations the Caernarfon jury failed to reach a verdict. Many Welsh supporters were elated at this outcome, but the authorities in London were alarmed. Finally it was decided that the trials of 'the Penyberth three' should be transferred to the Old Bailey in London.

At the London trial in January 1937, as most people expected, the three men were found guilty, and they were sentenced to nine months in Wormwood Scrubs, a sentence which many considered to be rather lenient considering the seriousness of the offence. However, this whole affair, and especially the transfer of the trials from Wales to England, inflamed Welsh passions to fever pitch and did much to galvanise Welsh nationalism. Lloyd George was incensed. He said, 'This is the first Government that has tried Wales at the Old Bailey...'

But that is not the end of the story. Many years later, just before the Penyberth nightwatchman died, he is alleged to have confessed to the minister of his Nefyn chapel that he had not been attacked on the night of the great Llŷn fire. He allegedly admitted that he was nowhere near the Air Ministry site when the fire was started but, instead of being at his watchman's post, he was half a mile away with his dog, poaching rabbits!

Urdd Gobaith Cymru at Porth Dinllaen

In the aftermath of the Great War there was much concern in some quarters for the future of the Welsh language. In many parts of Wales all areas of life outside the home and the chapel seemed to be increasingly dominated by English. Sir Ifan ab Owen Edwards commented, 'These days, in many villages, and in most towns in Wales, children play and read in English. They forget that they are Welsh.'[15] Sir Ifan ab Owen Edwards was a man who was determined to do what he could to safeguard the future of his native tongue. He decided to set up Urdd Gobaith Cymru, a Welsh national youth movement which would encourage children and young people to come together to embrace the Welsh language and have fun at the same time.

Inspired by his vision and hard work, the movement which he started spread rapidly in the 1920s, and local branches sprang up right across the country. Then in 1927 he established a tented summer camp where youngsters from all over Wales could spend time together. In 1932 Urdd established a permanent residential camp at Llangrannog in Cardiganshire.

A second tented camp was established at Porth Dinllaen in 1934 and, in the summer of that year, it accommodated 701 boys, the girls continuing to attend the Llangrannog site. The Porth Dinllaen camp site was a field belonging to Portinllaen Farm which was owned by Colonel Wynne-Finch of the Cefnamwlch Estate. At first Wynne-Finch objected to the Urdd camp coming to Porth Dinllaen. But correspondence in the Gwynedd Archives[16] reveals that, after he and his wife had visited the camp in August 1935, he was happy with what he saw. The following year he gave permission for Mr Griffith Jones of Edern to erect wooden huts in the camping field, and he agreed that those huts could be left in situ from one year to the next.

However, the Urdd camp at Portinllaen Farm was short lived. Just before the outbreak of the Second World War it was decided to close this camp, because the permanent site at Llangrannog had been extended to accommodate boys as well as girls.

After the war the Urdd movement continued to grow as more young people joined, and its activities were extended. Today it remains the chief youth movement in Wales with over 50,000 members. It promotes numerous activities, including sports and the Urdd Eisteddfod, to encourage young Welsh people to learn, socialise and enjoy themselves through the medium of the Welsh language. For a few years before the Second World War, Porth Dinllaen can claim to have played a small part in the history of this important Welsh-language youth movement.

Elizabeth Watkin-Jones, the Children's Author

Elizabeth Watkin-Jones, the Nefyn-born writer of children's books, was born on 13th July 1887, the only child of Captain Henry Parry and his wife, Jane. Hers was a seafaring family, for both her grandfathers were master mariners, and generations of her ancestors had also been sailors. Sadly, Elizabeth's father never saw his daughter. On 16th July 1888 he was swept from the deck of the iron barque *Gwynedd* as it approached the harbour of Iquique in South America, and he was never seen again. The family home was in Stryd Moreia, but it was at Tan Llan, the home of her maternal grandparents opposite the old Saint Mary's Church, that Elizabeth was born.

She was educated at Ysgol Nefyn and at Pwllheli County School. She spent a great deal of time with her maternal grandparents, and she seems to have been fascinated by the seafaring stories told by her grandfather, Captain David Davies, who had been master of the sailing ships *Slater* and *Polly Preston*.

At the age of 14 she moved to Mynytho to become a pupil teacher. Subsequently she gained a place at Bangor Normal College where she excelled in Welsh and History, and where she became President of the College Drama Society. Having qualified as a teacher, she taught younger children in South Wales before returning to Caernarfonshire to teach at Porthmadog and then at the Nefyn School.

Following her marriage to John Watkin-Jones in 1916, she lived in Merthyr for a few years before coming back to Nefyn in 1920, when her husband was appointed to the headship of the Nefyn School.

In those days married women were not allowed to remain in teaching, and so it was at her Nefyn home, before the Second World War, that she began to write stories for children. Her writing was undertaken in a very small room on the upper storey from where, at frequent intervals, she could walk out onto the balcony at the front of the house to gaze out over the sea.

At first she wrote short stories in English which were published in several children's magazines. Then she wrote contributions for a number of Welsh children's publications and comics. She also wrote a large number of scripts for BBC children's radio, and she penned plays which were performed by the children of Capel Soar, Nefyn. Several of her children's plays won prizes at the National Eisteddfod. In August 1940 it was stated that, for the 4th year in succession, she had won the prize for the children's play at the 'National'. In 1945 it was reported that she had won three prizes at the National Eisteddfod – 'for her children's story, for her children's drama and for her children's novel.'[17]

It is for her children's Welsh historical novels that Elizabeth Watkin-Jones is best remembered. Between 1939 and 1955 she wrote seven historical stories for children, and all but one were set in Nefyn. They included *Plant y Mynachdy* (1939) which was her own favourite, *Luned Bengoch* (1946), *Esyllt* (1951) and her last novel, *Lois* (1955). Before publishing her novels she would read them in serial form to the children at Capel Soar so that she could judge their reactions and, needless to say, those Nefyn children thoroughly enjoyed her story sessions.

Perhaps her most popular story was *Luned Bengoch* and, nearly four decades after it was first published, this novel was revised and updated by her nephew, Hugh D. Jones. Revised versions of three of her other stories have also been produced.

Elizabeth Watkin-Jones died on 9th June 1966, a few weeks before her 79th birthday. Following her death, her husband arranged for a gold crown to be made, and he presented it to Urdd Gobaith Cymru in memory of his wife. Today it is used to crown the main literary prize winner at the Urdd Eisteddfod each year.

Elizabeth Watkin-Jones's work has also been honoured in her home town of Nefyn. On the wall of the house where she lived, 'Garth' in Rhodfa'r Môr, a commemorative slate plaque has been erected by Cyfeillion Llŷn. It bears the inscription 'Llenor: Cymwynaswraig Plant' (*Writer: Benefactor to Children*) – a fitting tribute. Over the years thousands of Welsh children have enjoyed her writings and adventurous tales, and today she commands a place as one of the leading children's authors in the Welsh language.

Henry Parry of Montclare

Henry Parry, who was born at Muriau, Stryd y Plas, in December 1900, came from a seafaring family. His paternal grandfather was Captain William Parry, Waen, Morfa Nefyn, and his father, also named Henry, was a ship's master who served with the Canadian Pacific Railway Company and the Elder Dempster Company. By 1910 the family had moved to Caerau, Stryd y Ffynnon.

His obituary in the *Caernarfon and Denbigh Herald* provides details of his life and achievements. As a child young Henry was educated at Ysgol Nefyn and Towyn Residential School. It is not surprising that young Henry should have followed in the family tradition of a career at sea, and therefore, like his father, he joined the Canadian Pacific Line. He served in the Merchant Navy during the early part of the Great War, attaining the rank of First Officer, but he was forced, through ill health, to abandon his Merchant Navy career and seek a future elsewhere. He decided to go to Liverpool University to study dentistry. Having qualified, he returned to Nefyn to join the School Dental

Service, inspecting and treating the teeth of Llŷn school children. His home was 'Montclare' on the Morfa Road opposite Saint David's Church, a house which he named after one of his father's ships. During the later years of the Second World War he was the officer in charge of the Nefyn Home Guard with the rank of major. In 1960 ill-health forced him to retire prematurely from his dental work.

Despite his indifferent health he was a keen golfer – he was a past captain, vice-captain and president of the Nefyn and District Golf Club. He was also a founder member and the first secretary of the Nefyn and District British Legion. Throughout his life he was an ardent supporter of the lifeboats. He was a member of the Porth Dinllaen lifeboat crew for over 15 years, during which time 33 lives were saved, and in 1964 he produced a brochure to commemorate the centenary of the Porth Dinllaen lifeboat station. He also published two books about wreck and rescue along the coast of Wales – *The Lifeboats of Cardigan Bay and Anglesey* (1969) and *The Story of the North Wales Lifeboats* (1973).

Although his work in maintaining the health of children's teeth was very important, his most enduring efforts involved documenting the history of the area, especially its maritime past. He maintained a passion for local history throughout his life and, as a relatively young man, he began to gather together as much material relating to Nefyn's past as he could acquire. He amassed a vast collection of documents, articles, photographs, and postcards relating to Nefyn, as well as any other local maritime information and ephemera that he could lay his hands on. He also gathered together and recorded an enormous amount of detail about the maritime history of Llŷn and the general history of the peninsula. In his later years he participated in a number of radio and television programmes about historical aspects of life in Nefyn.

Today 'The Henry Parry Papers' constitute a very important resource in the Gwynedd Archives, Caernarfon, and many researchers who delve into local and family history have every reason to be grateful to Henry Parry for his diligence and foresight in preserving such a valuable body of archive material.

Following Henry Parry's death in February 1973 his ashes were scattered in the bay at Nefyn by members of the Porth Dinllaen lifeboat crew.

The Gough Family of Gorse Cliff

Gorse Cliff, now renamed Penrallt, is a substantial house situated half way between Nefyn and Morfa Nefyn. As early as 1910[18] it belonged to a wealthy Englishman, The Revd Prebendary Alfred William Gough MA, who was a canon of Saint Paul's Cathedral and the long-serving vicar of Holy Trinity Church, Brompton. Although he was a London vicar, he spent a considerable amount of time in Nefyn where, at one time, he was the captain of the golf club. Alfred Gough came from a family of clergy, for his father was The Revd Howard E. Tunnicliff Gough, four of whose five sons also became clergymen.

Born in Hartshill, Staffordshire, Alfred Gough was educated at the Merchant Taylor's School and Saint John's College, Oxford. He was an ardent supporter of the 1914-18 war against Germany, and when the British Workers' Party (a conservative pro-Great War patriotic labour movement) was founded in 1916 he became its chairman for London and the Home Counties.

In the 1920s he became particularly well-known for his tireless work as chairman of the Christian Protest Movement, a world-wide pressure group which fought against religious persecution in Communist Russia. One newspaper commented in his obituary, 'The fact that it (the cause) was taken up in almost every European country, as well as in America, was a tribute to his magnetic leadership.'[19] (*The Straits Times* 05/11/1931)

Following Alfred Gough's death in London in October 1931 and the death of his wife, Adeline, in February 1933, Gorse Cliff passed to their only surviving son, Fitzherbert Charles Gerald Gough who had been born in December 1899. Gerald, (as he was generally known) was educated at Eton and Balliol College, Oxford. He was a bachelor, and he seems to have lived a rather interesting life, although by his own admission it was not an altogether happy one.

After graduating from Oxford in 1922, he pursued a career in the Colonial Service, becoming Private Secretary and Aide-de-Camp to Herbert Stanley, the British Administrator and Governor of Northern Rhodesia. Subsequently he worked for both the Foreign Office and the Home Office.

His five scrap album diaries provide a fascinating insight into his career from about 1923 until just after the Second World War. They are full of photographs, postcards, newspaper cuttings, letters and jottings about his experiences. During his time in the Civil Service he travelled widely, visiting numerous places across the globe.

It is believed that, in the period leading up to the Second World War, he worked for the Foreign Office at the British Embassy in Berlin. His written observations about Nazi Germany in the 1930s are particularly interesting. He referred to the country as 'a fearfully policed state'; he observed that the German people were pre-occupied with the defeat inflicted upon them during the Great War; he stated that 'a worship of athletics seems to have taken the place of religion'; and he described German officials as 'tin-gods before whom humility is advisable'. He mentioned that he visited, among other places, the Brown House (Hitler's Nazi Party HQ in Munich), a concentration camp at Worms and a labour camp in East Prussia. He wrote about the 'bitterness of politics' in Germany, where he witnessed at first hand the struggle between Fascism and Communism. He reported that the Nazis and the Communists were killing each other on a daily basis. 'Large numbers of people say the trend must be either towards Moscow or Hitler', he wrote. 'Perhaps a middle party can steer a reasonable course.'

In his diary Gough also wrote, 'After I left the Home Office I went through a very unhappy period, brought upon me by the stupidity of others; only a kind of wry sense of humour brought me through.' During this period it is clear that Gough had some kind of involvement with MI5, the British Secret Service.

In one of his scrap albums there is a signed copy of a three-page, typed letter (undated but probably written in the late 1940s) addressed to Colonel W. H. Cooke, Room 055 at the MI5 Headquarters. The contents of that letter suggest, for reasons we can only speculate about, that Colonel Cooke probably dismissed Gough from a position at MI5 or possibly turned him down for a post within that organisation. Gerald Gough referred to 'the inquiry of 1940', but he provided no further details, although he subsequently mentioned that Cooke considered 'some of his contacts from long ago' undesirable.

It is clear that Cooke had made enquiries about Gough's activities. He had asked questions about three meetings between Gough and an Italian Fascist at Glan Conwy in 1938 as well as his contact with a German, whom he had met once. In his defence, Gough stressed that he had informed Colonel Cooke's representative about the Italian and he went on to state that he was 'the object of much hatred and suspicion to the Nazis'. He pointed out that he was arrested when he tried to cross the German border on the last occasion in 1937, and he mentioned an attack which he suffered in Yorkshire in 1939, two incidents which he admitted he should have reported to Colonel Cooke.

Gough's diaries also record that, some time after he left the Home Office, he eventually enlisted in the RAF where he worked in intelligence. After leaving the RAF he obtained a position with the United Nations Relief and Rehabilitation Administration (UNRRA), an organisation which had been set up in 1943 to relieve the suffering of war victims in both Europe and Asia.

In his letter to MI5, Gough referred to the unfair way in which Cooke had treated him. He stated that the MI5 Officer had tried to block his promotion in the RAF by suggesting that he should not be allowed access to confidential information. He also mentioned that he had been forced to resign from UNRRA because Cooke had sent an unfavourable report about him to that organisation.

One might infer from the contents of this letter that the MI5 officer was probably under the impression that Gough may have had secret underlying Nazi sympathies, and therefore was not to be trusted. This letter to Colonel Cooke appears to have been a last ditch attempt by Gerald Gough to clear his name with MI5. His diaries reveal that, having tried to set the record straight, he returned to Gorse Cliff from where he continued to travel the world. It would appear that Colonel Cooke was not the only person to look at Gerald Gough with raised eyebrows, for he seems to have been regarded as a rather eccentric character by many of the local Nefyn people. Gerald Gough died on 12th October, 1986 aged 86 years.

Notes
1. *CDH* 01/05/1925
2. *Illustrated Guide Book: Aberystwyth & North Wales* (Southern Edition) Ward Lock 1922-3
3. *NCW* 28/04/1922
4. *NWC* 17/03/1922
5. *C&DH* May 1924
6. *C&DH* 28/08/1925
7. *C&DH* 23/01/1925
8. *NLW* 08/12/1933
9. *CDH* 01/07/1927
10. 1880 Coastguard Journal of Thomas John Thomas, Bangor University Manuscripts
11. *C&DH* 07/04/1939
12. quoted by Aled Eames in *Ventures in Sail*
13. *C&DH* 17/08/1917
14. Press reports of the hearing at Pwllheli Magistrates Court (*C&DH* 18/09/1936) and the trial at Caernarfon Assizes (*C&DH* 16/10/1936) . Also details of the trial evidence in *Tân yn Llŷn* by Dafydd Jenkins
15. Urdd History on Urdd Gobaith Cymru website
16. Gwynedd Archives XD/32/648-652
17. *C&DH* 10/08/1945
18. Inland Revenue Land Valuation Book 1910 Gwynedd Archives XLTD/34
19. *The Straits Times* 05/11/1931

Chapter 5

The Second World War 1939-1945

Introduction
The slide towards war with Germany for a second time within the space of two decades filled everyone with dread, for painful memories of the last conflict were still vivid in the memory. In the Welsh heartland it is not surprising that the traditional pacifism came to the fore once more. In September 1939 there was no longer the same patriotic fervour that had existed at the start of the Great War; indeed there was now an air of desperation and resignation among the majority of the people.

As in 1914, some Welsh people adopted a determined anti-war stance, either on the grounds of conscience or because they felt that Wales was being dragged into war yet again by the Westminster Government. Moreover there was considerable opposition to conscription in Wales, just as there had been in 1916. This was particularly true of Llŷn where the influence of the chapels was still very strong. There was a huge anti-conscription rally in Pwllheli, and in May 1939 there were peace and anti-conscription meetings in Nefyn, at both Capel Isa and Capel Moreia.[1]

Without being euphoric about the prospect of another armed conflict others took a different view. They were of the opinion that the forces of totalitarianism must be confronted, for a hatred of Nazi ideology and grave suspicions of Hitler's formidable war machine were uppermost in their thoughts. The *Caernarfon and Denbigh Herald* expressed the view that Hitler was not to be trusted, and in June 1939 it stated, 'Conscription has come and it is long overdue.'[2]

During the 1930s, as Hitler and Mussolini became increasingly dangerous to the world order, Lloyd George, ever mindful of the appalling loss of life incurred during the previous conflict, had hoped that a peaceful way forward might be found. He had advocated the setting up of a European Peace Conference. However, by 1939 he appears to have accepted that war was inevitable. At the Nefyn Agricultural Show on Easter Monday 1939 he suggested that the British army, navy and air force must be strengthened immediately. He also stressed the important part which local agriculture would play in providing food for the population of the country in the event of war. 'We are in greater danger than we have been since 1918,' he said. 'Whatever happens, I ask people of all parties to stand firm for the old country.'[3]

As Lloyd George advocated, preparations for hostilities were already being made. Plans for conscription had been drawn up; gas masks were being produced in case poisonous gas was dropped on British towns and cities; plans for rationing were prepared; air raid precautions were made ready; arrangements were put in place to boost food production; organisations like The Red Cross, The Auxiliary Fire Service, The Saint John's Ambulance and The Women's Voluntary Service were mobilised; and rural areas like Llŷn were advised to expect a mass influx of child evacuees from urban centres such as Merseyside which would almost certainly be targeted by enemy bombers.

Once war had been declared people who were liable for military service were drafted into the armed forces. But all those people who remained at home were to play their part in the war effort, too. Nefyn men who were neither conscripted nor in the Merchant Navy were coerced into joining the Local Defence Volunteers (later renamed 'The Home Guard') or one of the other local civilian wartime organisations; and some young women from the parish joined the Women's Land Army to work on farms. Other local residents raised money to assist the war effort, while many Nefyn families looked after evacuees in their homes. As never before, this was to be a war fought by everyone and, confronted by a powerful common enemy, nationalistic differences were 'put on the back burner' for the time being.

In the early days of the war additional airfields were hastily constructed across the country, including several in North Wales (RAF Towyn 1940, RAF Bodorgan 1940, RAF Llandwrog 1940, RAF Valley 1941, RAF Llanbedr 1941); coastal defences were built; fortified defensive 'stop lines' consisting of concrete pill boxes, anti-tank barriers (similar to the one installed at the top of Lôn Gam) and defensive trenches (like those on top of the cliffs facing the sea at Nefyn) were hastily prepared; the country was ringed by a series of early warning radar stations, including RAF Nefyn; and Observer Corps posts, like the one established at Penbryn Holborn, were created to assist with the monitoring of all aircraft movements.

Throughout the war, even at the height of the Blitz, Nefyn remained relatively safe, although the hostilities certainly had a profound effect upon the town and parish. Young sailors from Nefyn and Morfa Nefyn, who were serving in the Merchant Navy, were engaged in extremely dangerous work; other local young men and women left home to join the armed forces or some other kind of wartime service; soldiers of various nationalities were stationed in Nefyn; military vehicles became a common sight in the district, which hitherto had been relatively free from motorised traffic; in addition to undertaking their daily paid employment, many local people served their communities during evenings and weekends as ARP Wardens, members of the Nefyn Local Defence Volunteer Force/Home Guard, Royal Observer Corps personnel, or members of the Auxiliary Fire Service and the Special Constabulary; many ladies of the parish focused their efforts on raising money to provide comforts for local men who were in the forces, as well as collecting funds for the general war effort; evacuees from Liverpool schools descended on Nefyn and Morfa Nefyn and were compulsorily billeted in people's houses; a prisoner of war camp was established on the Morfa Road at Glan Pwll; and it was not long before news began to filter through once again that local men had been killed or wounded, or had been captured and were now prisoners of war in foreign parts.

During the war there was a considerable amount of activity in the air above Llŷn. Many of the planes flying over the peninsula were RAF and Allied aircraft, for several of the local airfields were RAF training stations. Llŷn offered few vital targets for the Luftwaffe, although the airfield at Penrhos was attacked on a number of occasions during the early part the war, and several high explosive bombs were dropped in other parts of the peninsula. From time to time German planes flew over the coastal areas on reconnaissance missions, to drop mines in coastal waters or to attack allied shipping in the Irish Sea.

It must also be remembered that Caernarfonshire lay on the route taken by German bombers heading for Liverpool. Enemy planes would set off from airfields in north-western, enemy-occupied France, fly across the English Channel, and then head for Cardigan Bay before making for Merseyside. As a young child, R. Gerallt Jones remembered hearing the 'the heavy drone of aircraft overhead' and then 'creeping to the window to watch the searchlights swinging above and beyond Eryri.'

Altogether 25 men from Nefyn and Morfa village were to lose their lives in this conflict, and it was the merchant seamen of the parish who were to suffer the heaviest casualties, with a total of 19 sailors lost from the two communities. A replacement lifeboat for Porth Dinllaen was also a casualty of the war. In 1940 a new boat was being built for Porth Dinllaen in a boatyard at Cowes on the Isle of Wight when German bombs destroyed it along with two other lifeboats which were under construction. On many occasions during the war the Porth Dinllaen lifeboat was required to render assistance to British and Allied ships which had been attacked by enemy planes, or to search a location where an aircraft had plunged into the sea.

At this time many Nefyn people still firmly believed that Sunday ought to be a day of rest and worship. Consequently there was strong opposition in the town when the Air Ministry decided to carry out air gunnery and bombing practice on Sundays. In September 1941 there was also an outcry against the allocation of Sunday as the day set aside for Civil Defence exercises and for registering for fire fighting duties.[4] Full-scale warfare was not considered a sufficiently good reason to violate the Sabbath!

During the war Nefyn and Morfa Nefyn still possessed a considerable number of shops and trades people. For the most part, the people of the two communities shopped locally because very few families possessed a car and petrol was strictly rationed. Moreover, a shopping trip to Pwllheli by 'bus was very inconvenient, since it tended to occupy most of the day.

The 1942 *North Wales Directory* reveals that the two communities were served by three banks (Barclays, Midland and National Provincial), a bookseller, three bootmakers, a builder, four butchers, a chemist, a coal merchant, a dentist, three drapers, three fruiterers/greengrocers, nine grocers, a hairdresser, two ironmongers, three motor engineers/garages, a nurseryman, two riding schools and a tailor. There were also four private hotels in addition to the Nanhoron and the Sportsman, as well as 13 apartments and boarding houses to cater for visitors.

The war years were difficult and anxious times for everyone. In the early days people in Nefyn were convinced that a German invasion was imminent. Furthermore, throughout the war many Nefyn families were worried about loved ones who were away from home and exposed to danger; food was rationed and inevitably there were shortages; people were working long hours and, even in a rural district like Llŷn, they were forced to put up with numerous inconveniences.

When the war finally ended in 1945, after nearly six long years, there was great rejoicing, and local celebrations were held to mark the victories over both Germany and Japan. Soon young men and women began to return to Nefyn and Morfa after demobilisation from the forces, and they were welcomed home. Although wartime shortages and rationing continued during the immediate post-war period, life in Nefyn began to return to a semblance of normality. In May 1945 the Nefyn & District Golf Club held its first Whitsun golf competition since 1939;[5] in September 1945 'The Welcome Home Sheep Dog Trials' were held at Holborn Farm with about 60 dogs taking part, many of them international winners;[6] by November 1945 the 'Nevin Celts' are recorded playing competitive football again;[7] and the newly re-formed Nefyn Town Band made its first public appearance on Christmas Day 1945, when it paraded through the streets of the town under the leadership of Mr D. H. Hughes, Foelas.[8]

Protection against Invasion in the Nefyn Area

The Llŷn peninsula was not heavily fortified in the same way that the southern and eastern coasts of England were defended. However, it was felt that if Ireland was invaded by the Germans, an invasion of Wales from the west would almost certainly follow. Instructions were drawn up concerning the treatment of refugees from Ireland, and a number of defensive measures were put in place. In May 1940 the County Road Engineer was instructed to remove all the road signs throughout Caernarfonshire, since they might be helpful to infiltrators and invaders trying to find their way around the county. The Gwylwyr Quarry pier was destroyed in case the Germans attempted to use it during an invasion. R. Gerallt Jones recalled the concrete road blocks that had been installed at the top of Lôn Gam and he also mentioned the lines of trenches that were dug into the headland at Penrhyn Nefyn. Other trenches were dug into the fields of Penisa'r dre Farm, on top of the cliffs overlooking the sea.

The main routes to and from Nefyn were regularly patrolled by members of the 14th Battalion of the Royal Welch Fusiliers who were billeted in Nefyn, with their Officers' Mess in the Sportsman's Arms and the Mess for other ranks in the Madryn Hall.[9] The Government had commandeered both the Madryn Hall and the Church Hall for military use. During the war other army units were based in the town, including the Royal Irish Fusiliers and young Norwegian volunteers who had left enemy-occupied Norway so that they could be trained to participate in covert, commando-style operations in their homeland. These young Norwegian men proved to be particularly popular with the local people.

The Nefyn Home Guard

In the summer of 1940, with the threat of a German invasion looming, companies of men were formed across the country to defend their communities. At first they were called the Local Defence Volunteers or LDV. Some people jokingly maintained that these initials stood for "Look, Duck and Vanish". Initially the Nefyn Local Defence Volunteer Force (officially known as Group 9) totalled 147 men[10] and their commander was an Englishman, Captain O'Farrell MC of Cliff Castle. Group 9 was part of Zone 2 of the Caernarfonshire LDV. The LDV consisted of men who were either too old or too young to enlist in the armed services, as well as men in reserved occupations. Some of the older men had fought in previous conflicts.

In the summer of 1940 every Caernarfonshire family was handed a leaflet, printed in both Welsh and English. It explained exactly what civilians should do in the event of an invasion, and it provided detailed instructions concerning the action people should take if enemy parachutists descended near their homes. It seems that some members of the Caernarfonshire Home Guard became a little too enthusiastic when they saw parachutists floating down. Their immediate reaction was to blast the intruders from the sky, but unfortunately they did not always gets things right. On occasions they shot at parachuting British pilots by mistake, and therefore revised instructions had to be issued.[11]

Within a short space of time the name of the LDV was changed to 'The Home Guard' on the instructions of Prime Minister Winston Churchill. Home Guard personnel had to undertake 48 hours of training per month, and failure to enrol or turn up for parades and training could result in prosecution and a fine. In November 1942 a Nefyn Home Guard member was summoned to appear before Pwllheli magistrates for failing to attend Home Guard parade[12] and in January 1943 another Nefyn man was fined £2 with £2 50s costs by Pwllheli magistrates for failing to enrol in the Home Guard at the Church Hall on two separate occasions.[13]

After a time the Caernarfonshire Home Guard was reorganised into sectors. Under the new arrangement, Nefyn fell within the Snowdon Sector which was divided into battalions, and subdivided into companies. 'D' Company (the Nefyn Home Guard) was part of the 4th Battalion. At first the officer in charge of the 4th Battalion was Lieutenant-Colonel C. S. S. Curteis CMG DSO with his Battalion HQ at the Porthmadog Drill Hall. At this time the Nefyn 'D' Company was still under the command of Captain O'Farrell. R. Gerallt Jones recalls watching the men of the Nefyn Home Guard 'marching up and down in their patchwork uniforms' together with 'the moustachioed O'Farrell, with his brisk little steps, his silver topped cane and his incomprehensible accent' as he bawled out his orders.

By July 1943 O'Farrell had been promoted to Lieutenant-Colonel in charge of the 4th Battalion with its HQ at Hendre Gadredd, Cricieth. Henry Parry, the Nefyn dentist, was promoted to officer i/c the Nefyn 'D' Company with the rank of major. The Nefyn Home Guard headquarters was the Church Hall on the Morfa Road, and whenever a community function was held there it was always 'by kind permission of Colonel O'Farrell of the Home Guard'.

One of the tasks of the Nefyn Home Guard involved patrolling the coastal paths to guard against enemy agents infiltrating from the sea, and it was the strict rule that all local fishermen must notify the Home Guard if they would be coming ashore after dark. One extremely dark night, three Nefyn Home Guard members were patrolling the cliff top when they heard noises below. They stopped and listened. They could hear the muffled sound of oars dipping into the water. With knees knocking together they quietly cocked their rifles and pointed them into the darkness below. Then, with fingers trembling on the triggers, they waited. After a short period of time they heard the bottom of a boat slide onto the shore, and then the faint murmurings of indistinct voices. As the intruders drew nearer and nearer, the terrified Home Guard trio were convinced that they were about to be confronted by a couple of heavily-armed and ruthless enemy agents who had been sent ashore from a German U-boat in the bay. Suddenly, much to their relief, they could hear that those voices were speaking quietly in Welsh. The men coming towards them were just a pair of local fishermen who had forgotten to notify the authorities that they would be coming ashore after blackout.

At first, the Nefyn Home Guard undertook weapons training on the mountain near Carreg Lefain until one day a farmer's sheep was accidentally shot dead, after which the cliff top became the firearms practice area so that members could shoot towards the sea. Apparently, on one occasion, the Nefyn Home Guard personnel were on the cliff top when they noticed one or two seals bobbing about in the sea below them. Instantly they decided to take the opportunity to engage in some real-life target practice, and so they began to fire at the bobbing targets. Altogether they discharged about 2,000 rounds. The next day one dead seal was washed up on the Nefyn beach and, when the corpse was inspected, it was found to have been killed by a single bullet to the head. The fact that 1,999 rounds appeared to have missed their target was not exactly a ringing endorsement of the men's marksmanship!

However, by 1944 it appears that the company's skill with hand-held weapons had improved, for in June of that year a Snowdon Sector Home Guard Shooting Competition was staged. The 4th Battalion, which included the Nefyn Company, came second in the rifle shooting competition, and they won the light machine gun contest. Those taking part in the rifle shooting were 2nd Lieutenant G. Jones, Sergeants H. Ensor, J. Thomas, and R. J. Hughes, Corporals P. T. Dawson, W. Thomas, R. D. Lloyd, R. Griffiths, A. Jones and Edward Jones. Those in the LMG competition were Sergeant Paine, and Privates H. Williams and J. Jones.[14] The awards were presented by the Sector Commander, Colonel R. J. Wordsworth, DSO, TD.

Not all the efforts of the Nefyn Home Guard were devoted to protecting the shores of their homeland. In February 1941 they arranged a very successful musical concert in the Madryn Hall with Mr Idris Lewis presiding. There were contributions from the Nefyn and Llangwnadl choirs, and solos by Trefor Hicks and Fusilier Jones, as well as community singing.[15]

The Telephone Cable Hut at Abergeirch and the Repeater Station in

Morfa Nefyn were considered to be vulnerable wartime targets. Throughout the war they were guarded by the 2nd Cheshire (GPO) Battalion Home Guard under the command of Major F. Baldwin. A total of eight men were detailed for this duty, three at the Abergeirch Cable Hut, three at the Repeater Station in Morfa village and two for reserve and relief duties.[16]

Air-Raid Precautions

From the outbreak of war, in order to protect the public from enemy bombers, the Government stipulated that no lights must be shown during the hours of darkness. This was known as 'the blackout'. Windows had to be covered by thick blackout curtains or blinds, and wardens walked the streets after dark to ensure that no lights were shining from the houses. Sometimes those infringing the regulations would be reported and prosecuted. In February 1941 a Morfa Nefyn resident was summoned to appear before the Pwllheli court, accused of 'displaying unobscured lights'.[17] He was found guilty and fined ten shillings. In June 1941 a female Nefyn resident was fined £1 for displaying a light after dark.[18] The blackout times were advertised regularly in the local press.

The blackout brought increased danger to those who were walking after dark, and the number of road accidents soared dramatically, especially those involving pedestrians in urban areas. The dangers were less acute in rural areas where the volume of traffic was relatively light. However, Llŷn was not without its dangers when people were walking in the pitch blackness. One Friday night in August 1940 a young couple from Morfa Nefyn had a narrow escape when they set off late in the evening to walk home from a dance in the Pwllheli Legion Hall. They lost their way in the darkness and had the misfortune to stumble into the town's inner harbour. Their cries for help were heard by a passing soldier who jumped, fully clothed, into the water whilst another man threw a rope. Fortunately, on this occasion, no one came to any permanent harm.[19]

When children were at school their teachers were responsible for implementing the Air-Raid Precautions. Since most local schools did not possess purpose-built air-raid shelters the Ysgol Morfa Nefyn log book records that teachers were required to identify a nearby field which contained hedges and ditches or in which trenches could be dug. In the event of an emergency the children were to be scattered around the field under the hedges and in the ditches so that everyone would be kept safe if a stray bomb fell nearby. If there was insufficient time to evacuate the building the children were to be instructed to lie flat on the classroom floor well away from the windows in order to avoid injury by flying glass.

The Royal Observer Corps

The Royal Observer Corps was composed mainly of part-time civilian volunteers who had been trained in aircraft identification. Observer personnel wore RAF-style uniforms and they were issued with high-powered naval binoculars. Their job was to watch for, and to report, any movements of aircraft within their area, to notify the authorities of possible aircraft crashes and to log changes in the weather conditions. Observer posts, which were manned both by day and by night, were usually situated 10-15 miles apart in order to afford adequate coverage of the country.

The Nefyn Observer Post was situated at the top of the town at Penbryn Holborn. Known officially as F1, the Nefyn post was part of 282 Observer Group which also included the posts at Chwilog (F2), Bangor (B1), Capel Curig (C1), Ceunant (G1), Penygroes (G2), and Porthmadog (G3).[20] Observers were required to be on duty for at least 24 hours each week, although they could be required to be present for 48 hours if necessary. Reports from the Nefyn Observer Post were sent through to Group HQ at 31 Bangor Street in Caernarfon so that, if any enemy aircraft had been spotted entering the area, planes from Fighter Command could be alerted.

Although there is no record of enemy planes striking at Nefyn, there were several incidents, during the early part of the war, when places nearby in Llŷn were attacked. Reg Chambers Jones has listed the raids for the month of October 1940. Bombs were dropped on RAF Penrhos on five separate occasions during that month, and the station was also machine-gunned several times; on one occasion a train was machine-gunned as it approached Pwllheli station and four nearby farms were also attacked; high explosive bombs fell in Rhydyclafdy, Efailnewydd, Llanbedrog and near Tudweiliog; incendiaries were dropped on parts of Pwllheli, Abersoch and Llanbedrog; and one day a German plane machine-gunned Y Maes in Pwllheli, damaging several shop fronts.

RAF Nefyn

During the 1930s, as Hitler became a greater danger, there were voices in Britain clamouring for a sophisticated scientific defence system to protect their shores against air attack. For a number of years scientists had been experimenting with an early warning system, using radio wave technology which could penetrate low cloud cover and look into the far distance in order to detect incoming enemy bombers. And so the first radar early warning system was born. By the spring of 1939 twenty-two radar stations had been built and were operational on the East and South-East coasts of England.

In a surprisingly short time other radar stations were constructed, until eventually a string of almost 200 such bases ringed the shores of these islands from Cornwall to the Shetlands. These radar stations were codenamed 'Chain Home'. Two miles from Y Bryncynan on the road which leads to Dinas there is a farm called Cefn Leisiog. On the land surrounding that farm a Chain Home radar station was constructed during the early part of the war. That station, RAF Nefyn (Air Ministry Experimental Station Number 66), became operational in September 1940.

There was another Home Chain station in Llŷn, at Pen y Bryn above Aberdaron, on the end of the peninsula. These two Llŷn radar stations were part of the western chain of defences, covering the approaches to Merseyside and protecting shipping in the Irish Sea. They were the responsibility of Number 9 Group Fighter Command whose headquarters were at RAF Barton Hall near Preston. Early warning enabled fighter pilots to scramble quickly in order to deal with the approaching threat.

There were two types of Chain Home station. RAF Nefyn was a Type 1 station which was able to provide long range detection but which could not detect aircraft flying in at low levels. The RAF also constructed Chain Home Type 2 stations, like RAF Pen y Bryn (also known as Chain Home Low or CHL stations). Type 2 stations did not have long range detection capabilities but they were able to identify aircraft flying as low as 500 feet. Therefore RAF Nefyn (a long range Type 1 station) and RAF Pen y Bryn (a short range Type 2 station) complemented each other to provide complete radar coverage of the Llŷn Peninsula.

The equipment employed at these radar stations was very primitive by modern standards, but it was surprisingly successful in determining the distance, altitude, direction and numbers of incoming enemy 'planes. RAF Nefyn consisted of substantial wooden pylons interspersed with taller, thinner ones constructed of metal. One type of pylon received the incoming signals while the others were transmission masts. Both kinds of masts were anchored to the ground by large square blocks of concrete, and between the masts stretched the radio antennae.

Signals of approaching planes were received in the Chain Home station control room where RAF personnel (usually members of the Women's Auxiliary Air Force or WAAFs) sat in front of display screens linked to the receiving equipment. Theirs was highly skilled and important work which demanded intense concentration. They noted the range, bearing and number of the 'blips' on the screens and converted them to a grid reference. This information was passed to the filter room at Group Fighter Command HQ where the incoming threat was plotted by staff on a huge map. These details were then passed to the Group Operations Room from where fighter squadrons were notified so that they could scramble. It was usually possible for a radar station to provide 24 minutes warning of incoming enemy planes, sufficient time for a squadron to become airborne, and then climb to the optimum height for launching their attack.

Today, on the land around Cefn Leisiog Farm, one can still see some of the concrete bases which supported the masts, several grass-covered bunkers, a tower and certain other buildings, some of which are now being used as domestic accommodation.

RAF Nefyn appears to have escaped bombardment by German aircraft, although there was an incident on October 3rd 1940 when the newly-constructed station was almost certainly the intended target. On that evening at dusk a lone German bomber flew in and dropped a stick of ten bombs which fell harmlessly just south of Tudweiliog. It has to be assumed that RAF Nefyn was the intended target.

Evacuees from Liverpool

In certain urban areas, considered especially vulnerable to airborne attack, entire schools (children together with their teachers) were evacuated. North Wales became the evacuation destination for large numbers of children from the densely-populated areas of Liverpool, Bootle, Birkenhead and Wallasey, all of which were considered to be at great risk. The evacuees were billeted with local families, who were required by law to accept them if they had sufficient accommodation available. Local newspapers record that one or two Nefyn folk failed to comply with the requirements of the billeting orders, and they were summoned to appear before the Pwllheli magistrates.

The weekly billeting rates paid to host families were increased in May 1940 from 8s 6d to 10s 6d (for 10-14 year olds), 10s 6d to 12s 6d (for 14-16 year olds) and from 10s 6d to 15s 0d (young people over 16 years).[21]

Early in the war 100 children from Anfield Road School, Liverpool, arrived in Nefyn in the care of their teachers. The evacuees, who were given their schooling separately from the local children, were taught by their own teachers in the Nefyn chapel schoolrooms. By October 1943 all but seven of the Liverpool evacuees had returned home, and the one remaining teacher, Miss Freda Laskar, left Nefyn during that month. The seven evacuees who remained behind were absorbed into the Nefyn Central School.[22]

On February 13th, 1941 a class of children from Rathbone Road School Liverpool, in the care of Miss Pritchard, began work at Ysgol Morfa Nefyn where extra desks had to be provided. It is recorded that a couple of months later Mrs Wright Disgwylfa, the local ARP Warden, visited the school to inspect the children's gas masks.

Inevitably mass evacuation caused a great upheaval, not only for the evacuees and their parents but also for the host families in the reception areas. At first some evacuees had considerable difficulty in settling down in Nefyn because they were homesick and they found everything in their new surroundings strange, including the language and the rural quietness. There were those who missed their families and the noise and bustle of city life to such an extent that they became rather difficult to manage. There were some Nefyn families who experienced difficulty looking after children from the poorer parts of a large English city. Some were forced to cope with problems such as infestations of lice, bed-wetting, impetigo and scabies, poor hygiene, lack of good manners, unusual eating habits and inadequate footwear and clothing.

However, it must be stressed that many evacuees settled into their temporary homes very well, and some made lasting friendships with their foster parents as well as with local children. R. Gerallt Jones recorded how, from 1940 until 1942, his best friends were a couple of Liverpool evacuees called Philip and Roger. Initially, communication between them must have been extremely interesting because Gerallt spoke nothing but Welsh, while his two friends spoke only 'Scouse English'. However, during that friendship, Gerallt learned to speak some English while the two evacuees acquired a rudimentary Welsh vocabulary.

Naturally, from the outset there was much anxiety among the local population about with the prospect of having large numbers of English children foisted upon them. There were fears, as Mr J. T. Jarrett pointed out, that if all the available accommodation was filled with evacuees it would have a detrimental effect upon the tourist trade in Nefyn during the summer months.[23]

More importantly, there were fears that such an influx of English-speaking children would have an adverse effect upon the Welsh language locally. However, in March 1943, Dr Elfed Thomas, Director of Education for Caernarfonshire, stated, 'The danger of the evacuation system to Welsh culture has been grossly exaggerated, if indeed it existed at all. The presence of evacuated children in Welsh rural areas does not constitute a menace to the preservation of the Welsh language.'[24] He pointed out that 'education in Caernarfonshire had suffered little' from the presence of evacuees, who had benefited considerably by their experiences, especially in terms of their physical health and religious life.

In fact, like Gerallt's friends Philip and Roger, many evacuees quickly learned to speak Welsh, and some became so competent that they were able to participate in local eisteddfodau. The *Liverpool Daily Post* proudly reported in April 1941 that a party of evacuees from Anfield had won the party-recitation competition at an eisteddfod arranged by the Nefyn and District Sunday School Union. On another occasion a party of children were standing on the platform at Liverpool's Lime Street Station where they were heard singing most beautifully. Passers-by stopped to listen, but they were unable to understand the words that were being sung. They were convinced that it must be a choir of refugee children from France, Holland or Belgium. But no! They were Liverpool evacuees returning home from Llŷn, and they were simply passing the time by singing that old Welsh hymn, 'Calon Lân'.

The vast majority of local people made every effort to make the stay of their evacuees as happy as possible and, as Jill Wallis points out, 'in the rural district of Lleyn evacuees were met with great kindness.' On Boxing Day 1941 the local Nefyn WVS arranged a Christmas party for 90 evacuees, and toys and sweets were distributed. On New Year's Day 1942 the children were given another treat by the local WVS when gifts, sent by the Liverpool Local Education Authority, were distributed by one of the teachers dressed up as Father Christmas. On these occasions 'Mrs Lloyd Cliff Castle presided, assisted by Mrs West, Mrs Rosemary Rees, Mrs Owen Williams, Mrs Jones Brynmor, Mrs Jones Voelas, Miss Nancy Griffith Muriau, Miss Jones Llys Olwen, Miss Johnson Pwll Crwn, Mrs Makingson Cliffe Lodge, Mrs Griffith Edern, Mrs Lewis Uwch y Don, Mrs Harry Parry and Miss Haf Morgan Morfa Nefyn.' It is recorded that 'the children thoroughly enjoyed themselves and they were very grateful to kind friends and especially to the WVS.'[25]

The Liverpool children had been sent to a safe area so that they would not come to any harm. Nevertheless, there were instances of evacuees meeting with accidents. In July 1941 a Merseyside evacuee, billeted at Plas Tirion, Morfa Nefyn, was knocked down by a vehicle, but luckily he was not seriously injured. The outcome was far less fortunate for a Nefyn evacuee who was knocked down by an army lorry and tragically killed.

Other evacuees sometimes landed their host families in trouble with the authorities. Without seeking permission, a girl evacuee from Morfa Nefyn took the family's dog rabbiting while her foster mother was visiting Bangor. As the girl and the dog were crossing a field the dog began to chase sheep, and this was witnessed by a local resident who reported the matter to the police. Subsequently the owner of the dog was summoned to appear before the Pwllheli magistrates who fined her 35 shillings and ordered that the dog should be destroyed.[26]

In 1944, when Allied troops were massing on the English South Coast in preparation for the D-Day landings, children living in the south of England were evacuated, and the children from Starts Hill School, Farnborough, were sent to Morfa Nefyn. One of those children has since recalled that she had a wonderful time during her stay in Llŷn. She lived with Mr & Mrs Morgan in a small terraced house in Morfa Nefyn where she was treated with great kindness. Since she was learning to play the piano Mr & Mrs Morgan allowed her to practise on 'their wonderful old organ in their front room'. She went to Morfa Nefyn School; she learned to speak some Welsh; each Sunday she went to chapel where she sang in Welsh; she came third in a Welsh singing competition; she played on the rocks and on the beach at Porth Dinllaen; and she picked wild flowers in the winding lanes. She recalls that she was so happy that she was never homesick at any time during her stay in Morfa Nefyn.

Her experience was far from unique. As Jill Wallis points out, many former child evacuees who were sent to this part of Wales during the war were able to look back upon their experience with great fondness, and consequently their stay in these parts 70 years ago was the start of a genuine love of the Nefyn area which remained with them for the rest of their lives.

Lord Haw Haw and Enemy Spies
During the war people in Britain often listened to 'enemy propaganda wireless broadcasts' from a German radio station based in Hamburg. The broadcaster always began with the words, 'Germany calling! Germany calling!' and that person was known throughout Britain by the nickname of 'Lord Haw Haw'. His purpose in making those broadcasts was to undermine the confidence of the British people and to sap their spirit, and at first these broadcasts did cause some concern among the population. However, after a while many folk began to dismiss his outbursts and threats, and he became the object of much ridicule throughout the United Kingdom.

Sometimes Lord Haw Haw referred specifically to Wales and, as R. Gerallt Jones recalls, on one occasion he mentioned Porth Dinllaen as a suitable landing place for a German invasion. He also stated that Boduan Woods would be an excellent hiding place for the invading army. This broadcast did cause some anxiety locally, and for some time afterwards local people would cast nervous glances in the direction of Boduan woods whenever they hurried past on foot or on bicycle, especially after dark!

From the beginning of the war it was feared that enemy agents might infiltrate the country, and detailed instructions were laid down for the apprehension and treatment of people suspected of being enemy aliens. Government slogans like, "Careless Talk Costs Lives" reinforced the possibility that there might be subversive elements within our communities, and many rumours about spies began to circulate around the Nefyn area.

One such rumour prevalent in Nefyn at the time was that there was a German spy living in an isolated wooden hut further along the coast towards Carreg y Llam. The spy was reputed to be either a female or a man disguised as a female. On occasions this person was seen walking around Nefyn accompanied by several dogs. It was also rumoured that a light had been spotted shining out to sea from the area near Carreg y Llam – firm evidence, so people thought, that someone was communicating with an enemy U-boat lying in the bay.

One day the stranger purchased a can of paraffin from one of the shops in Nefyn, and the following day the wooden hut in which he or she had been living was burned to the ground. When the police sifted through the wreckage at the site they found evidence of dogs' bones among the burned-out debris, but no trace of human bones. The stranger was never seen again. To this day nobody knows who that person was or what happened to him or her!

The Prisoner of War Camp in Nefyn
Early in the war, Nefyn was one of seven unit collecting points in the region where prisoners of war could be housed prior to being sent to the sub area 'cage' at Wrexham. According to documents in the Gwynedd Archives, prisoners of war held at Nefyn were guarded by 'E' Company of the 14th Battalion Royal Welch Fusiliers. If no road or rail transport was available to take the prisoners to Wrexham they would be force-marched via Porthmadog, Ffestiniog, Bala and Bryneglwys before reaching their destination. Those places were to be night halts, and the Home Guard companies at those locations were to be responsible for providing food and for reinforcing the soldiers who were acting as escorts.

Eventually three prisoner of war camps were established in Llŷn, one at Nefyn and the others at Sarn and Chwilog. The Nefyn POW camp was situated on the Morfa Road where the council houses were subsequently built at Glan Pwll. This camp consisted of several corrugated-iron Nissen huts, erected in a small field which was surrounded by a high wire fence. R. Gerallt Jones recollects riding past this camp on his bike and glancing at the Italian prisoners 'drifting around behind high fences.' Later on, it housed German prisoners of war.

Enemy prisoners were well treated and they were granted a considerable amount of freedom towards the end of the war. Many were set to work on local farms and after the war had ended several German prisoners decided to remain in Nefyn. One or two former prisoners married Nefyn girls, they were accepted into the local community and they lived out the rest of their lives within the town. One such person was Siegfried Nierada who married local girl, Megan. He worked very hard to establish a garage on the Morfa Road. He became a very successful businessman and a well-respected member of the local community.

Aircraft and Shipping Incidents in the Nefyn Area

Several aircraft came down in the vicinity of Nefyn during the war. Henry Parry recalls that the busiest year for the Porth Dinllaen lifeboat was 1941. During that year it was launched no fewer than ten times to go to the aid of aircraft which had crashed into the sea, although it was required to render assistance on just one of those occasions.

At the beginning of the hostilities an RAF Hurricane, serving with one of the locally-based squadrons, suffered engine failure whilst flying over Nefyn Bay. The 21 year old pilot, having decided to make an emergency landing, took his plane downwards in a steep dive. Unfortunately he missed his intended landing site and one of the plane's wings struck a large rock on the beach causing the aircraft to flip over. The 'plane finally came to rest upside down in the sea fairly close to the beach. Local people, who rushed to help the pilot, eventually managed to turn the plane over with the aid of several sturdy wooden planks but there was no sign of the pilot. Some time later, when the tide had gone out, a policeman noticed a hand protruding from the sand. The pilot's body had sunk out of sight into the soft wet sand. Rescuers managed to recover the body and it was very quickly removed from the beach.

As a young child, R. Gerallt Jones watched a German bomber fleeing from an RAF fighter 'plane. The enemy aircraft finally crashed into the mountainside at Garn Fadryn. When the bodies of the aircrew had been removed by the Local Defence Volunteers, and after the military had inspected the shattered remains of the German 'plane, Gerallt and his friends climbed up to the scene of the crash. There he discovered, and took away, an instrument dial and a small piece of the plane's fuselage upon which a fragment of the painted German swastika could be seen. When he reached home with his wartime treasures he was severely admonished by his clergyman father for looting a crash site!

In January 1942 an RAF Whitley Mark V aircraft was on a training mission over the Irish Sea when engine failure caused the trainee pilot to make for the nearest land. The plane eventually crash-landed onto the headland at Morfa Nefyn near the golf course. Unhurt, the pilot, together with his instructor, walked to the Linksway Hotel in Morfa Nefyn where the owners, Mr and Mrs Lane, treated them to an appetising hot dinner.

Another British plane, a De Haviland Mosquito, plunged into the sea off Nefyn on October 11th 1944. Records reveal that the French lifeboat, *Jean Charcot*, which was temporarily in service at Porth Dinllaen at the time, was despatched to search the scene together with an RAF rescue launch, and one body was recovered at 1.30 pm. In 2001 a local fisherman dredged up some engine parts which were subsequently identified as components from an aero engine. A local diver went down to investigate and he discovered the remains of the Mosquito. One of the plane's two engines has since been recovered together with a propeller, and both are now in the aircraft museum at Dinas Dinlle.

On July 23rd 1944 Lieutenant Ben Brew of the US Air Force was in his P-47C Thunderbolt fighter aircraft, returning to base at Atcham, Shropshire. He had been practising dog fighting over the Irish Sea with the 52nd Fighter Training Squadron, and when he did not return to base he was reported missing. Many years later an aeroplane engine of the type used in Thunderbolts was dredged up in a fishing net off Nefyn – almost certainly one of the engines from Lieutenant Brew's plane.

A number of ships were bombed and machine-gunned by enemy aircraft off the northern coast of Llŷn. In March 1941 the SS Iris of Amsterdam was reported to be on fire 19 miles south west of Porth Dinllaen. She had been attacked by enemy aircraft off Ynys Enlli. The Porth Dinllaen lifeboat went to her assistance and a lifeboatman was put on board the stricken vessel to pilot her back to Porth Dinllaen, where an injured crew member was landed so that he could be transferred to the Bryn Beryl Naval Hospital, a few miles away.

In December 1941 the lifeboat was called out to the British tanker, *Lucellum*, which had been attacked and set on fire by the Luftwaffe, also off Ynys Enlli. The Porth Dinllaen lifeboat and a naval patrol vessel could see no sign of life aboard the burning tanker but they continued to search the area all night looking for survivors. Subsequently it was discovered that several members of the *Lucellum*'s crew had managed to reach Holyhead. In 1942 the steamer *Knut* hit a mine off Ynys Enlli and sank. The 15 crew members scrambled into a ship's lifeboat, and eventually came ashore at Porth Dinllaen.

At some stage during the war, possibly prior to the Normandy landings in 1944, the bay at Porth Dinllaen was used for allied beach-landing exercises, using amphibious craft which could travel on land as well as through the water.[27] During the war mines were a constant danger in the coastal shipping lanes. In 1942 several mines were washed up on the northern coast of Llŷn. One such mine came ashore in the middle of Nefyn Bay. It was quickly made safe but, for several years afterwards, its outer casing remained in the middle of the beach where it provided an exciting piece of equipment on which children could climb. Eventually the metal case became corroded by the salt water and it disappeared into the sand. On another occasion a mine was washed onto rocks near Carreg y Llam where it blew up with such a massive explosion that it could be heard several miles away. Fortunately, because the mine had come ashore in a remote location, it caused no personal injury and no damage to property.

The Voluntary Services and Fund Raising
The voluntary services, as well as various Nefyn groups and local individuals, played a very important part in fundraising during the war. Groups were formed to provide comforts for soldiers. In 1940 a garden fete at Cliff Castle, organised by the Weekly Knitting Group, raised over £52 towards the Services' Comforts Fund.[28] In February 1941 a concert in the Madryn Hall was arranged by Corporal Parry in aid of comforts for members of the forces.[29] The Knitting Group, meeting weekly in the Legion Hall, also provided comforts for the Home Guard.[30] The Nefyn Red Cross, led by their Commandant Mrs Trenholme Garn View, raised money for the 'Prisoners of War Fund' and also collected for the Penny-a-Week Fund.[31] The pupils and staff of Nefyn Central School raised money in December 1943 so that they could provide Christmas gifts for Nefyn seamen who were prisoners of war.[32]

Other monies were raised to assist the war effort. A house-to-house collection in aid of the 'County Spitfire Fund' was organised by Mrs Sleigh of Cliff Castle, whose husband was a Squadron Leader.[33] Mrs Williams, Sarnllys, and her War Savings Committee, organised a house-to-house collection in aid of the 'Wings for Victory' Campaign,[34] while in four months during 1941 they collected nearly £800 by selling sixpenny and half crown National Savings Stamps.[35] In 1944 the Women's Groups in Nefyn and Morfa Nefyn raised a huge sum of money by undertaking house-to-house collections for the 'Salute the Soldier' Campaign.

Not all their fund-raising efforts were in aid of their own folk or the war effort. In October 1940 a collection from the Soar, Isa and Moreia chapels, was handed over to the East End of London Relief Fund.[36] This money was destined to assist those unfortunate folk in the East End of London who had suffered so grievously during the London Blitz. In 1945, when the war was almost over, the ladies of Nefyn decided to carry on knitting so that garments could be sent to the needy people in recently-liberated countries on the continent of Europe.

Agriculture and Food

Although in 1939 there were still many farms in rural parishes like Nefyn, about 60% of the food required to feed the people of these islands was imported. When war was declared farmers were urged to boost agricultural production once again. County War Agricultural Executive Committees were established to oversee food production. The Caernarfonshire Committee issued regular instructions and advice to farmers within the county, and if a farmer refused to carry out the committee's instructions he risked having his land requisitioned. Some Nefyn young women enlisted as wartime 'land girls' to work on farms, and subsequently prisoners of war were also deployed as farm workers locally.

In order to ensure an equitable distribution of essential foodstuffs, rationing was introduced at the beginning of the war, and information concerning the issue of new ration books was printed from time to time in the local newspapers. The successful 'Dig for Victory' campaign helped to boost food production at home. Rural communities like Nefyn fared much better for food than people in most urban areas, since rural houses and cottages tended to have larger gardens where produce could be grown and where poultry could be kept. Some older rural properties also had a pig sty where a pig could be fattened.

Furthermore, there were other valuable food sources readily available. Blackberries could be gathered for jam-making, and large numbers of wild rabbits were caught for food. The practice of catching rabbits not only provided an excellent source of free meat, but it also helped to eradicate a pest which destroyed valuable crops.[37] Local fish provided another source of nourishing food. There are many references in the *Caernarfon and Denbigh Herald* to huge hauls of fish at Nefyn during the war. In July 1940 it was reported that 'a large catch of mackerel was made on Monday by Mr Hugh Williams, Conservative Club'.[38] The next year Nefyn fishermen netted 600 herrings[39] while in July 1942 a very good haul of mackerel at Nefyn was reported, the first of the season.[40] Later that year, the fishermen of Nefyn enjoyed '... a record haul of 3,000 mackerel. This is the third big catch of the last two months'.[41]

Wartime recipes were broadcast on the radio, and cookery hints were printed regularly in the local newspapers. In July 1940 'four "Wartime Cookery Lectures" were given at the Nefyn Central School by Mrs Alice Jones. The chair was taken by Mrs Owen Williams, Sarnllys, and the hostesses were Mrs Roberts Maes Rhyg and Mrs Parry, Montclare.'[42] In October 1940 three wartime cookery demonstrations were given by Miss Jane Roberts at Nefyn Central School. Such events were organised by Caernarfonshire Education

Committee in co-operation with the Ministry of Food.[43] Because there was a shortage of certain types of food it was essential that children maintained a healthy diet. The Ysgol Morfa Nefyn log book records that certain local children were given free cod liver oil and iron tablets to supplement their diets.

During the war it was almost impossible to acquire some foreign foodstuffs like oranges and bananas. One morning, news reached a group of youngsters who were waiting at the bus stop in Nefyn that a large quantity of oranges had been washed up on the beach. Instantly they set off down Lôn Gam and, as soon as they turned the corner, they could see that there were scores of oranges scattered along the waterline, obviously part of the cargo from a wrecked ship. The sight of those oranges during wartime must have seemed like manna from heaven! Quickly they hurried down to the beach where they began to sample those tempting fruits. Having removed part of the peel, they bit into the juicy flesh only to find that it tasted so awful they were forced to spit it out immediately. Everyone was convinced that the oranges had been in the salt water for such a long time that they had gone completely rotten. Little did they know that those foul-tasting fruits were in fact extremely bitter Seville oranges, suitable only for making marmalade!

Wartime Cultural Life and Entertainment
During the war the radio was one of the main sources of home entertainment, while people were kept informed about the progress of the war via regular radio news bulletins. For local men and women in the armed services certain broadcast programmes provided them with a link to home. One Friday afternoon in January 1945 a BBC van arrived at the Nefyn Central School to record items for 'The Welsh Half Hour Programme'. The children were recorded singing Welsh folk songs, and Doctor O. Wynne Griffiths of Pwllheli, who had been a pupil at the opening of the Nefyn Board School in 1868, 'delivered greetings to the Nefyn boys and girls who were serving in the forces'.[44]

Despite the war, there were frequent social and cultural events in Nefyn. There were regular meetings of the various chapel literary societies, as well as concerts and plays featuring local talent, eisteddfodau, singing festivals, beetle drives, whist drives, meetings of the Nefyn and Morfa Women's Institutes and dances in the Church Hall or the Madryn Hall, with music provided by the Glyn Williams Band from Pwllheli.[45]

Despite Mr Jarrett's concerns about evacuees occupying all the accommodation for holiday-makers, the war did not appear to restrict visitors to the area. On 1st August 1941 the *Caernarfon and Denbigh Herald* reported that there were many visitors staying in the Nefyn district over the weekend. In July 1943 it was stated that 'the influx of visitors to Nefyn and Morfa Nefyn this year exceeded all records of previous years.'[46]

The Welcome Home and Victory Celebrations

In August 1944 a Nefyn committee was formed to make arrangements for the home-coming of local men and women who had been serving in the armed forces. The officers of the committee were Councillor Humphrey Evans, Siop Newydd (Chairman), Mr Idris Lewis, Midland Bank (Treasurer), and The Revd W. H. Rowlands, Baptist Chapel (Secretary). Great efforts were made to raise funds for the 'Welcome Home'. For example in August 1945 a sale, organised by Nefyn and Morfa Nefyn WVS, the Red Cross and the Welcome Home Committee, was held at Nefyn Central School and the sum of £253 was raised.[47] In September 1945 a Welcome Home Concert was held at Capel Isa. The chairman was Mr R. Roberts, Derwen and the compère was Mr T. Hughes, London House. A male voice choir, conducted by Mr E. Williams, took part.[48]

Victory in Europe (VE Day) was celebrated in Nefyn with flags and bunting decorating the streets. Thanksgiving services were held at Saint David's Parish Church, as well as at Capel Moreia and Capel Isa, arranged under the auspices of the Evangelical Church Council. There was community singing on the square and bonfires were lit at Penrallt.[49]

To celebrate victory over Japan (VJ Day) arrangements were made to entertain all the children in the parish to a tea party at the Nefyn Central School, followed by a carnival and sports in a field near the Nanhoron Hotel by kind permission of Mr & Mrs G. H. Parry. In the evening an open air dance was held and the master of ceremonies was Major Owen Roberts. The music was provided via a radiogram, and the field was floodlit from the Nanhoron Hotel.[50]

Local Personnel who Served in the Armed Forces during World War II

Many Nefyn and Morfa men and women served in the armed forces during the Second World War. They served in all branches of the services and in all theatres of war – at Dunkirk, in the Far East, in North Africa, in Italy, during the Normandy landings, in Holland and in Germany.

Sometimes they were mentioned in the local press because they had been taken prisoner – for example, Private Harry Parry, Talyllyn, had been reported missing but was later discovered to be a POW in Germany, having been captured in Belgium; Private Richard Jones, Brynarfor, was a POW for four years; Sergeant Pilot Gwilym Griffiths, Plevna, was taken prisoner in 1943.

Other soldiers and airmen were mentioned in the newspapers because they had been wounded – Guardsman Owen Jones, Belle View, was wounded at Dunkirk and he spent three months in a military hospital; LAC E. Roberts, Tegfryn was wounded in Italy; Private E. Davies, Tan y Bracty was wounded during exercises in England; Major C. A. Manning (Royal Artillery) Ryefield and Private J. Evans Maes y Ddôl, were both wounded during the Normandy beach landings; Gunner Robert Jones Glynllifon Terrace, was wounded in Holland; Privates J. G. Thomas Fron Terrace, and D. Wynne Williams, Madryn View, Cefn Morfa were both wounded during the final advance through Germany.

The two parish war memorials record the names of six local soldiers and airmen who lost their lives in World War II:

Harry John Jones Frondeg aged 19 Fusilier 7th Battalion Royal Welch Fusiliers Service No. 14716787 Killed in action in Germany 14/02/1945 Son of Mr and Mrs Jones of Nefyn Buried in Reichswald Forest War Cemetery

Griffith E. Owen Gwalia aged 22 Aircraftsman Royal Air Force Volunteer Reserve Service No. 1667476 Died of wounds received in action 11/09/1944 Son of Mr and Mrs R, R, Owen Nefyn Buried in Nefyn New Cemetery

Rees Gwyn Owen Sunnyside Lieutenant A volunteer regular soldier Killed in action in 1944 Son of Mrs Elizabeth Owen and the late Mr Rhys Owen of Morfa Nefyn Recorded in Nefyn New cemetery No further details known

Owen Lewis Roberts Tyn y Cae aged 24 Fusilier 1st Battalion Royal Welch Fusiliers Service No. 4193442 Killed in action in Burma 18/03/1943 Son of Mrs A. S. H. Blore of Nefyn Buried in Taukkyan War Cemetery Burma

D Williams Fron Oleu Killed in action during the Second World War No further details known

Owen Emrys Williams Cae Bach aged 19 Private 4th Battalion Welsh Regiment Service No. 14410986 Killed in action in Normandy 23/07/1944 Son of Catherine Williams and the late Thomas Williams of Morfa Nefyn Buried in Banneville-La-Campagne War Cemetery France

Nefyn and Morfa Merchant Seamen who Served in World War II
During the war many men from the parish served in the Merchant Marine. Once again they were charged with the vital task of bringing essential

materials and goods to this country as well as transporting troops and supplies to theatres of war around the world. This was highly dangerous work, for German U-boats and surface warships were continually seeking to destroy British and Allied merchant ships wherever they could find them. British merchantmen were also at the mercy of floating German mines, and they were frequently attacked from the air by enemy aircraft.

Most supply ships travelled in convoy, perhaps as many as forty or fifty vessels sailing together. Although there was a certain degree of safety in large numbers, sometimes convoys were decimated by enemy U-boats hunting in wolf packs. This was the experience of Captain Sam K. Williams of Morfa Nefyn, Chief Officer on the *SS Zarian*, which was part of a convoy bound for West Africa with war materials. The convoy was attacked by U-boats in mid Atlantic, his ship was one of 17 vessels torpedoed and, after a desperate struggle for survival on a life raft, he was eventually picked up by a British destroyer.[51]

Several merchant sailors were captured and interned as prisoners of war. Included among that number were: Engineer Thomas Henry Parry Garth y Don, who spent nearly five years in captivity after his ship was torpedoed and sunk off the Norwegian coast in June 1940; Officer T. H. Parry Glanydon was a prisoner for four years; Captain Evan Davies Hafan, Morfa Nefyn, was reported missing for five months after his ship, *MV Dalhousie*, had been torpedoed in the South Atlantic in August 1942, but he was later discovered to be in a German prison camp in northern Germany; Ellis Hugh Jones had not been heard of for several months until it was discovered that he was a prisoner in East Africa; Captain John Griffith Jones Afallon, Morfa Nefyn, was a prisoner of the Japanese for three years, an ordeal which he managed to survive; Captain Owen Robyns-Owen was also a prisoner of the Japanese in Manila, but he was less fortunate. In January 1945, a few months before the end of the war with Japan, he was brutally bludgeoned to death by one of his prison guards.

One of the most hazardous missions for seamen during the war was to participate in the Arctic convoys which sailed the northern passage to the ports of Archangel and Murmansk. This was the route taken by ships supplying the beleaguered Russians, and such convoys suffered many casualties in the icy waters of the Arctic. One such victim was Captain Hugh Williams, formerly of Gwynfryn, Nefyn, but later residing in Pwllheli; and another was Captain William Williams Primrose Villa, Morfa Nefyn. Both went down with their ships in northern waters when their vessels were sunk by German U-boats.

The sailors who worked on tankers performed a vital role in bringing fuel to these shores, but such a ship was extremely dangerous, especially when fully laden. One Nefyn sailor who served on tankers was Thomas David Davies Isfryn. One night German submarines penetrated the harbour at Aruba in the Dutch West Indies where scores of tankers, including Thomas's ship, were at anchor. That night every tanker in the harbour was torpedoed and set ablaze. Hundreds of sailors, including Thomas, were blown up or burned to death in that inferno. Captain William Roberts Ancon, whose large tanker was also torpedoed and sunk during the war, was so traumatised by the experience that he never went to sea again but obtained employment as a local coastguard. Captain Richard Griffiths Llysarborth, whose father had lost his life when his ship was torpedoed during the Great War, was a tanker captain for the Shell Company throughout the Second World War and beyond. Apprentice John Lewis Jones Police Station, Nefyn, had a lucky escape when his tanker *SS San Demetrio* was set on fire, but more will be said of his story in due course.

The following Merchant Seamen from Nefyn and Morfa lost their lives during this conflict:

Thomas D. Davies Isfryn Aged 41 Second Officer on *SS Oranjestad* (London) Lost 16/02/1942 Son of Mrs Jane Davies and late Captain William Davies of Nefyn and brother of Captain Robert Davies, Preswylfa

Robert J. Davies Glan y Ddôl Aged 29 Carpenter on *MV Athelking* (Liverpool) Lost 09/09/1940 Son of William and Maggie Davies & nephew of Jane Davies of Nefyn

Richard G. Evans Bay View Aged 44 Chief Engineer on *MV. Siamese Prince* (London) Lost 17/02/1941 Son of William and Ruth Evans Husband of Jane Evans of Nefyn

Emrys Griffith Minafon Aged 31 Able Seaman on *SS Almenara* (Glasgow) Lost 20/09/1943 Son of William and Elizabeth Griffiths of Nefyn

Richard O. Griffith Maes Gwyn Aged 45 Chief Officer on *SS Montreal City* (Bristol) Lost 21/12/1942 Husband of Ann E. Griffith of Nefyn

Eliseus Griffith Jones Angorfa Aged 65 Second Officer (Master Mariner) on *SS Ulea* (Glasgow) Lost 28/10/1941 Husband of Mrs M. G. Jones of Morfa Nefyn

R. J. Jones Arosfa Lost his life due to enemy action in the Second World War Son of Lewis and Jane Jones of Morfa Nefyn No further details known

Thomas Idris Jones Talyllyn Aged 24 Carpenter on *SS Aguila* (Liverpool) Lost 19/08/1941 Son of Thomas and Mary Jones of Morfa Nefyn

Owen Robyns-Owen Gwynle Aged 67 Chief Officer on *SS Seztan* (Hong

Kong) Died in captivity at hands of Japanese 09/01/1945   Son of John and Catherine Robyns-Owen   Husband of Myfanwy Robyns-Owen of Morfa Nefyn

G. C. Roberts   Bryn y Ddôl   Aged 26   Seaman   Lost at sea in 1943   Son of Mr and Mrs G. Roberts of Stryd y Llan, Nefyn

David A. Rowlands   Plas   Aged 22   Seaman on *MV The Lady Mostyn* (Chester)   Died 23/07/1940   Son of David John and Elizabeth Rowlands of Nefyn

John V. Rowlands   Plas   Aged 31   Second Officer   *SS Normandy* (Liverpool)   Died 11/01/1945   Son of Mrs Elizabeth Rowlands of Nefyn

Edwin Griffith Williams   Glanmorfa   Aged 23   Carpenter on *SS Marlene* (London)   Died 04/04/1941   Son of Ellen Jane Jones of Morfa Nefyn

Owen G. Williams   Bodfel   Aged 49   Mate on *MV The Lady Mostyn* (Chester)   Died 23/07/1940   Husband of Mrs Mary Williams of Nefyn

Thomas J. Williams   Bodfel   Aged 16   Cabin Boy on *MV The Lady Mostyn* (Chester)   Died 23/07/1940   Son of Owen G. (above) and Mary Williams of Nefyn

William Williams   Primrose Villa   Aged 54   Master of *SS Empire Gilbert* (Sunderland)   Died 02/11/1942   Husband of Mrs M. Williams of Morfa Nefyn

William H. Williams   Bodfel   Aged 27   Able Seaman on *SS Marcella* (London)   Died 13/03/1943   Son of late Owen G. and Mary Williams of Nefyn

Some of the Local Men were Commended during the War
Able Seaman W. E. Hughes, Ealing House, who was serving with the Royal Navy, 'was honoured by the admiralty for bravery and devotion to duty', but the newspaper report fails to give any further details.[52] **Captain William Williams**, Primrose Villa, was posthumously mentioned in despatches, 'For great bravery and devotion to duty in carrying supplies to North Russia.' **Captain T. R. Wilson**, Summer Hill, Nefyn, received a letter of thanks from the Admiralty for saving his ship from enemy attack, as reported in the *Caernarfon and Denbigh Herald*:

> Captain T. R. Wilson, Summerhill, Nevin, is home on a few days' leave. He has received a letter from the Admiralty thanking him for his services in saving his ship from enemy attack a short time ago. Captain Wilson said that one moonlit night, soon after midnight, his ship was attacked by enemy planes. One of the planes swooped down low to attack and came within range of the ship's anti-aircraft

and machine gun fire, and in a few moments a shell found its target. In order to regain height the attacker released bombs which fell into the sea not very far from the ship. The bomber then crashed into the sea and the crew of four bailed out and were rescued from their dinghy and taken prisoner. Half an hour later another plane attacked, but received a hot reception and was damaged so that it had to turn away. Two other attacking planes were chased away by anti-aircraft fire and cleared away. This lively encounter lasted for three hours. The ship suffered no damage and there were no casualties among the crew. The ship proceeded on its way and arrived safely in an English port."[53]

Lieutenant Gwilym H. Davies of the Royal Artillery, the younger brother of John Ifor Davies, saw active service in both North Africa and Italy. It was while he was serving in Italy that he was awarded the Military Cross for gallantry. Under heavy enemy mortar fire, and at great personal risk, he saved the lives of several of his wounded men by carrying them to safety.[55] He was subsequently promoted to the rank of captain. Sgt. Harry Fray (RAF), Sportsman Hotel, was mentioned in despatches 'for services rendered, an honour which entitled him to wear the Bronze Oak Leaf.'[56]

Apprentice John Lewis Jones
John Lewis Jones, the 20 year old son of PC Richard & Mrs Jones, Police Station, Nefyn, was awarded the Order of the British Empire for Meritorious Service, and a Lloyd's War Medal for Gallantry at Sea. His ship, the oil tanker *SS San Demetrio*, was a member of the famous *Jervis Bay* convoy which was attacked in mid Atlantic on 5th November 1940 by the German pocket battleship *Admiral Scheer*. Despite the gallant efforts of *HMS Jervis Bay*, an armed merchant cruiser which was protecting the convoy, several ships were sunk including the *Jervis Bay* herself. When the *San Demetrio* was shelled and set on fire her crew members were forced to abandon ship.

They spent a terrifying night in two lifeboats, with heavy seas breaking over them and shells exploding overhead. When dawn broke Lewis Jones, together with the other crew members in his lifeboat, decided to return to their badly-damaged tanker which was still afloat, and for five hours they fought the fires which were still raging on board. Having extinguished the flames, they eventually managed to revive the ship's engines, and then they set sail eastwards across the Atlantic without a compass or chart, hoping that they would reach the safety of Ireland or Scotland rather than the coast of enemy-occupied France. After a journey of 500 miles and within sight of land, Lewis Jones painted 'SOS' in huge white letters on the front of the ship's bridge, and after a while the *San Demetrio* entered a bay to rest up for the night. Early the next morning the tanker was spotted by a patrolling RAF 'plane, and some time later a British destroyer, *HMS Arrow*, arrived to escort them into a port on the River Clyde where they were able to discharge 11,000 tons of their original 11,200 ton cargo of oil.

Subsequently, having already received his OBE from the King, John Lewis Jones was presented with his Lloyd's Medal at a special ceremony in the Madryn Hall. In front of a packed audience Councillor Humphrey Evans remarked that Apprentice Jones's 'heroic act had not only brought credit upon himself but also upon his native village.'[54]

The following extract, taken from the citation which accompanied his Lloyd's Medal, sums up the role which the young apprentice played in saving his ship and its cargo:

> Apprentice Jones helped to navigate the vessel without books, instruments, charts or compass. He kept alternate watches. He was one of those who offered to accompany the chief engineer to the gas-filled pump room. He proved a most capable second in command. It was mainly due to the efforts of the Chief Engineer and Apprentice Jones that the ship was brought into port and most of her valuable cargo was saved.

In 1943 the story of the *San Demetrio* was made into a film by Ealing Studios. J. Lewis Jones went on to become a Merchant Navy captain, with a career at sea which lasted until 1971. He lived at 'Highways', Morfa Nefyn until his death in 1986.

Sub-Lieutenant Michael Wynn RNVR

The Wynn family of Glynllifon and Boduan had been one of the most important landowning families in the Nefyn area for hundreds of years. A son of the family was Robert Charles Michael Vaughan Wynn, later to become 7th Baron Newborough. In 1940 and 1942 he took part in two of the most famous episodes of the Second World War – the evacuation of British and Allied troops from Dunkirk, and the raid on the strategic enemy-held French harbour of St Nazaire.

Michael Wynn was invalided out of the army early in 1940, but in the spring of same year hundreds of thousands of troops, including the British Expeditionary Force and thousands of French soldiers, were trapped on the French coast at Dunkirk by the encircling German army. Whilst detachments of soldiers fought a rearguard action, a desperate evacuation of the main body of troops was organised, and this involved over 800 ships and boats, including a great many small craft like fishing boats, yachts, pleasure cruisers and lifeboats. Altogether, from 27th May to 4th June, nearly 350,000 soldiers were evacuated from the harbour and beaches at Dunkirk, while the German Luftwaffe bombed and machine-gunned them. The Dunkirk evacuation was later described by Churchill as 'a miracle of deliverance.'

As a civilian, Michael Wynn made five successful trips to Dunkirk to carry troops back across the Channel until his yacht was disabled by shellfire. He then took command of a Norfolk fishing boat which he sailed to the beaches south of Calais to search for the members of a Guards regiment who were thought to be hiding in the sand dunes there.

In view of the courage and ability Wynn had shown at Dunkirk he was offered a commission in the Royal Naval Volunteer Reserve, and two years later Sub-lieutenant Michael Wynn RNVR participated in one of the most daring missions of the war – the raid (code-named 'Operation Chariot') on the harbour of St Nazaire, a vitally important naval port in German-occupied France. The Atlantic port of St Nazaire contained the huge *SS Normandie* dock, which was large enough to accommodate the giant German battleship *Tirpitz* and which was also an important German submarine base, from which U-boats set out to attack Allied shipping in the Atlantic.

In March 1942 Wynn's motor torpedo boat was part of a large flotilla of vessels which set off from the Cornish port of Falmouth, bound for St Nazaire. Their mission was to destroy both the new and the old gates of the huge Normandie dock. On reaching their target, an old destroyer, *HMS Campbeltown*, which had been packed with high explosives, was run at full speed into the new main gates of the dock. Small groups of commandos leapt ashore with instructions to blow up defensive positions. Wynn's motor torpedo boat fired its torpedoes at the secondary target – the old gates of the basin.

Everything seemed to be going according to plan but, as Wynn's torpedo boat was making its getaway, it stopped to pick up some survivors who were clinging to a life raft. While the motor boat was stationary two German shells ripped through it, and Sub-Lieutenant Wynn was hurled from the bridge with such force that he lost an eye and was knocked unconscious. His life was saved by Petty Officer Lovegrove, his chief mechanic, who dragged him onto a life raft. Twelve hours later Wynn and his surviving crew members were picked up by the Germans and taken prisoner. After a timed delay the *Campbeltown* exploded and two days later Wynn's two torpedoes also detonated. The dock at St Nazaire had been rendered totally unserviceable.

Wynn was sent to a prison camp near Bremen in northern Germany from where he escaped. He was subsequently recaptured and sent to the notorious POW camp at Colditz, where, in January 1945, he feigned serious illness so successfully that he tricked the Germans into repatriating him back to Britain.

For his role in the attack on St Nazaire Wynn was awarded the Distinguished Service Cross. At the end of the war, on hearing that Petty Officer Lovegrove was being held in a German naval prison, Wynn volunteered to be part of the relieving force so that he could greet the man who had saved his life at St Nazaire.

Wynn seems to have retained some of his adventurous spirit and daring attitude in later life too. On the occasion of his mother-in-law's birthday he is alleged to have celebrated by firing a 9 lb cannon ball across the Menai Strait from Fort Belan, which had been built by his ancestors during the Napoleonic Wars in the late 18th century. Unfortunately, the heavy missile smashed through the sails of a passing yacht, and Wynn was fined by the local magistrates for causing criminal damage. He died on 11th October, 1998.

Several books have been written about the raid on St Nazaire, and it was the subject of the 1968 film, 'Attack on the Iron Coast', made by Mirisch Films and starring Lloyd Bridges. Two documentary films, telling the story of this audacious operation, were screened on BBC television in 1973 and 2007.

Notes
1. C&DH 19/05/1939 & 26/05/1939
2. C&DH 02/06/1939
3. C&DH 14/04/1939
4. C&DH 19/09/1941
5. C&DH 18/05/1945
6. C&DH 28/09/1945
7. C&DH 08/11/1945
8. C&DH 28/12/1945
9. Gwynedd Archives XM/1301
10. Gwynedd Archives XM/1301
11. Gwynedd Archives XM/1301
12. C&DH 13/11/1942
13. C&DH 08/01/1943
14. C&DH 09/06/1944
15. C&DH 21/02/1941
16. Gwynedd Archives XM/1301
17. C&DH 07/02/1941
18. C&DH 13/06/1941

19. *C&DH* 160/8/1940
20. Gwynedd Archives XM/1301
21. *C&DH* 17/05/1940
22. *C&DH* 08/10/1943
23. *C&DH* 15/03/1940
24. *NWC* 08/03/1940
25. *C&DH* 02/01/1942
26. *C&DH* 27/06/1941
27. This was recalled by the brother of Dr Brian Owen who grew up in Nefyn during the war
28. *C&DH* 19/07/1940
29. *C&DH* 28/02/1941
30. *C&DH* 22/091940
31. *C&DH* 29/01/1943
32. *C&DH* 03/12/1943
33. *C&DH* 04/10/1940
34. *C&DH* 07/05/1943
35. *C&DH* 17/10/1941
36. *C&DH* 25/10/1940
37. *C&DH* 23/01/1944
38. *C&DH* 05/07/1940
39. *C&DH* 03/10/1941
40. *C&DH* 10/07/1942
41. *C&DH* 25/12/1942
42. *C&DH* 05/07/1940
43. *C&DH* 18/10/1940
44. *C&DH* 12/01/1945
45. *C&DH* 22/08/1940, 18/10/1940 & 10/04/1942
46. *C&DH* 23/07/1943
47. *C&DH* 13/04/1945
48. *C&DH* 28/09/1945
49. *C&DH* 11/05/1945
50. *C&DH* 12/08/1945
51. Account in Rhiw.com
52. *C&DH* 04/04/1941
53. *C&DH* 26/09/1941
54. *C&DH* 03/10/1941
55. *C&DH* 09/02/1945
56. *C&DH* 28/07/1944

Chapter 6

The Post-Second World War Years: 1945 – Present

Introduction
The Allied victory was greeted with scenes of great jubilation across the country, but the war had taken its toll. Many families had lost loved ones (including several Nefyn families), Britain was drained financially and the immediate post-war period was one of austerity, for rationing remained in place until 1954. In the decades that followed, Nefyn changed a great deal.

After the 1960s a 'buy-now-pay-later' consumerist attitude took hold on society, as people sought to acquire all the trappings of modern day living. This resulted in huge life style changes, which the inhabitants of Nefyn could never have imagined 130 years ago. Central heating, using electric storage heaters or bottled gas, was introduced into many Nefyn homes. Age-old daily chores were rendered obsolete by the acquisition of new household appliances such as electric washing machines, dishwashers, refrigerators, deep freezers, cookers, microwaves and vacuum cleaners.

After the 1960s, cars became a much more common sight within the parish, and today most households own at least one vehicle. Inevitably car parking presents considerable problems in a town where the roads evolved long before the invention of the internal combustion engine. Since the 1950s the availability of cheaper television sets and the proliferation of TV channels has completely transformed home entertainment. During the Second World War very few Nefyn homes possessed a telephone but, in the decades that followed, the domestic telephone, the home computer, access to the internet, the mobile 'phone and the smart 'phone have all revolutionised communication.

A few mariners from the Nefyn parish continued with a career at sea after the war. They included men like Captain Merfyn Evans of Moneifion, Morfa Nefyn, who gained his master's ticket in 1949, Captain Rowland Davies of Fernlea, Stryd y Ffynnon, Captain Edward Evans Rhys Everitt, Morfa Nefyn, Captain Samuel K. Williams Ivy Dale, Morfa Nefyn and Captain J. Lewis Jones Highways, Morfa Nefyn. Although comparatively few local men earned their livelihood in the Merchant Navy in the post-war period, the town still abounded with many retired captains and sailors who could be heard recounting fascinating stories about their days at sea. Today the merchant seamen of Nefyn and Morfa are simply part of the parish's rich history. The large number of fishing boats which once worked from Porth Nefyn have almost disappeared too, for only a handful of boats now remain, fishing mainly for whelks to supply the Far Eastern market.

Porth Dinllaen received a new lifeboat in March 1949. Named the *Charles Henry Ashley*, it was a 46 ft 'Watson' class craft, and it served at the station for 30 years. Two other lifeboats followed – the *Kathleen Mary* (1979-1987), a 47 ft Watson class vessel, and the *Hetty Rampton* (1987 – present), a 47 ft 'Tyne' class boat. In 2011 the station is due to receive a new 'Tamar' class lifeboat, and certain alterations are currently being made to the station in readiness for its arrival.

Since the end of the war, farming has moved forward both technologically and scientifically, but now there are relatively few farms within the parish, and very few people are employed on the land. Local farmers have experienced mixed fortunes during this period. For a time, following Britain's entry into the European Common Market, they prospered as subsidies boosted their incomes. From the mid 1980s onwards Welsh farming fell into decline; many smaller farms ceased to exist as working farms, while others sought additional revenue from sources like tourism. A series of disasters during the period added to their problems – the fall out from the 1986 Chernobyl nuclear tragedy continues to affect the sheep farmers of North Wales, while the 2001 foot and mouth epidemic prohibited farmers from selling and moving their livestock. Although most of the Nefyn farms have now disappeared, Llŷn remains essentially an agricultural area, and, as has already been mentioned, the Nefyn and District Agricultural Show continues to be an event which local people look forward to each year.

In 1945 the Nefyn British Legion decided to submit questions to the prospective Parliamentary candidates at the General Election concerning the possibility of reopening of the Gwylwyr Quarry. The intention was that it would produce granite kerb stones, thus providing work for local quarrymen returning from the forces.[1] However, their vision came to nothing and the quarry never reopened.

Since the end of the war both Nefyn and Morfa have witnessed a great deal of house-building, which has had a major impact upon the character of the area. This has included council houses, like the development at Glan Pwll (which, as already noted, was built on fields previously used as a prisoner of war camp) as well as private estates such as Bro Gwylwyr in Nefyn. There has also been quite a lot of 'in-fill' housing. In 1955 Nefyn was provided with its own purpose-built public library and a fire station. As mentioned previously, the Madryn Hall was no longer considered fit for purpose and so it was replaced by a new Nefyn community centre on the Morfa Road, but that too was demolished and rebuilt in 2010. In Morfa Nefyn the old Village Institute was replaced by a new community centre. In 2007 Nefyn was also provided with a new modern health care centre.

During the past 60 years the number of shops in Nefyn has dwindled as people have become more mobile. Most of the old shops have disappeared, and the town is now served by one bank, the post office, the printers/newsagents, the chemist, the hardware shop, a fish and chip shop, two hairdressers and one small but well-stocked supermarket. There are also several restaurants and cafes. In Morfa there is a fish and chip shop, a post office, a general store on the opposite side of the road and 'The Cliffs' restaurant.

Today Ysgol Nefyn is a Primary school rather than an all age Central School. Ysgol Morfa Nefyn retains its pupils until the age of eight when they transfer to the school in Nefyn. Since the introduction of comprehensive secondary education in the late 1960's children no longer sit the scholarship examination, for today there is no longer a grammar school in Pwllheli. At 11 years of age the children transfer from Ysgol Nefyn to comprehensive secondary school at either Pwllheli or Botwnnog.

The post war years have been marked by a steady secularisation of society. Immediately after the war many Nefyn folk still attended chapel or church each Sunday. Since then, the Sunday congregations have fallen away dramatically, and many of the chapels have been forced to close or reduce the size of their buildings. In Nefyn the large Calvinistic Methodist Chapel in Stryd y Ffynnon was demolished to be replaced by a much smaller modern building, more in keeping with the size of its congregation. The fine building that was the Baptist Capel Seion closed in 2001 while the Wesleyan Methodist Capel Moreia has also closed very recently. In Morfa village Tabernacl (the Congregational chapel) closed in the late 1960s and has since been converted into a dwelling. Caersalem (the Baptist chapel) closed its doors for the last time towards the end of 2003, while Capel Pisgah on Mynydd Nefyn has also closed and is now a dwelling. Those chapels which remain open for worship no longer attract the huge congregations of the 1880s and 1890s.

In the period following the Second World War the annual holiday became commonplace, and holidays with pay boosted the local tourist industry. The Nefyn area continued to attract family groups as well as walkers, golfers and the boating fraternity. The heyday of the Nefyn seaside holiday was the 1950s to the 1970s when large numbers of Nefyn folk took in paying guests during the season or hired out their houses and cottages to holiday-makers, retreating with their own families to a caravan or a chalet in the back garden. In the early 1960s Mr David Sutcliffe reintroduced film shows to Nefyn, and during the summer season talking films were shown in the town until about 1973. During this period many visitors to Nefyn remember seeing such films as 'The Dambusters' in the Madryn Hall whilst they were on holiday.

In more recent times, despite the longer season, the inexpensive foreign package holiday has dealt a blow to the traditional seaside holiday in resorts like Nefyn. Although the local businesses depend to a considerable extent upon the seasonal tourist trade, the influx of holiday makers at the height of the season does pose a number of problems locally. Today, the once popular seaside holiday in rented private houses and guest houses has largely given way to holidays spent at the local caravan and camping sites, and in holiday homes. A few hotels remain, such as the Nanhoron Arms and the Caeau Capel Hotel in Nefyn, and the Fairways Country Hotel in Morfa Nefyn. Recently the Linksway Hotel in Morfa was converted into holiday apartments.

During this period further evidence has come to light concerning the history of the area. The discovery of an Irish gold bracelet dating from the 9th century BC, found on a local beach, bears testimony to the migration to Llŷn of Celtic tribes from across the Irish Sea, and their settlement in the area. In 2010 it was discovered that, inside the Nefyn watchtower (built about 1846 in connection with the herring fishing), there was a blocked-up chamber, and old town records have indicated that it was formerly used as a lock-up for detaining local drunks.[2] The mount on which the present tower stands is the remains of a Norman motte and bailey castle – nearly five hundred of these earth and timber structures were built in Wales during the Norman attacks. The Nefyn castle was taken by the Welsh king, Gruffudd ap Cynan in 1094 and the Normans were driven out of Gwynedd.

Since the end of the Second World War there has been a heightened feeling in Wales that Welsh culture is being eroded, and efforts have been made to obtain greater recognition for Welsh national identity. During this period, in many parts of Wales, Welsh nationalist sentiment has manifested itself in a variety of forms of direct action, ranging from civil disobedience and the daubing of slogans to more destructive forms of expression. Nefyn has witnessed a number of such incidents, as we shall see later in this chapter.

Politically, the situation in Wales has changed dramatically since 1945. In January of that year Lloyd George, the long-serving Member of Parliament for the Caernarfon Boroughs (including Nefyn), was elevated to the Upper House with the title 'Earl Lloyd George of Dwyfor', but he died about two months later without ever taking his seat. For some time the Labour Party had been growing in strength, especially in the industrial areas of Wales, Scotland and England, and at the 1945 General Election Clement Attlee won a landslide victory. However, the Caernarfon Boroughs remained steadfastly Liberal, with Labour coming third in the constituency. Attlee, a regular visitor to Nefyn each summer, now became Prime Minister and leader of a reforming Labour government.

Plaid Cymru, *the Welsh Nationalist Party*, which hitherto had been a pressure group rather than a mainstream political party, barely survived the war. But in the decades that followed the end of the war, as Welsh national consciousness came to the fore, the National Party gradually increased its membership until at the 1974 General Election three Plaid Members were returned to Westminster, including the member elected to represent the constituency which included Nefyn. Subsequently the Westminster Government was forced to take greater notice of Welsh national feeling, and in 1979 and 1997 the people of Wales were offered referenda on a measure of home rule.

At the 1997 referendum Wales voted 'Yes', and in 1999 the National Assenbly for Wales was created. The people of Nefyn are currently represented by Plaid Members at both Cardiff and Westminster. On 3rd March 2011, by a referendum majority of 70% throughout Wales, the National Assembly was given the right to enact primary legislation without referring to, or asking consent from, Westminster. Undoubtedly further powers will be devolved to the National Assembly in future.

For centuries the Welsh language had been under threat in many parts of Wales, not only due to the inward migration of English people and the outward migration of native Welsh speakers but also as a result of legislation which promoted English as the dominant and official language.

From the middle of the 20th century, as the English language encroached more and more upon Welsh society, concern for the Welsh language grew, and attempts to safeguard its future became more urgent. In 1950, for the first time, Welsh became the sole and official language at the National Eisteddfod. In 1956 the spelling of the town's name was changed officially from 'Nevin' to 'Nefyn'.[3] A determination to ensure the survival of the language has resulted in the establishment of movements and institutions like Cymdeithas yr Iaith Gymraeg (*The Welsh Language Society*), Bwrdd yr Iaith Gymraeg (*The Welsh Language Board*), Merched y Wawr (the Welsh-speaking equivalent of the Women's Institute which has groups in both Nefyn and Morfa), Welsh language radio and television channels, and the Welsh Books Council. Crucial to the preservation of the Welsh language, with its strong literary tradition, has been Welsh medium education in nurseries, schools and higher education. For many centuries English was the language used for official purposes in Wales, but today official notices and documents are published in both Welsh and English. The establishment of the Welsh Assembly Government with its bilingual policy has given further impetus to the language.

Furthermore, Welsh learner language courses (such as those held at Drws Agored in Nefyn), the establishment of the Language Centre at Nant Gwrtheyrn in Llŷn in the 1980's, Welsh-language sites on the internet, and choirs, singers and entertainers who perform almost exclusively in Welsh have all played their part in ensuring that Welsh has a future. Locally, Llŷn has its own monthly community Welsh language newspaper, *Llanw Llŷn*, which was first published in 1977. Therefore today the people of Wales – and particularly those living in places like Nefyn where the vast majority (78.6% in 2001) of the population are Welsh speakers – are able to live their lives almost entirely through the medium of their national language. Efforts to protect and preserve one of Europe's oldest languages are on-going, and in 2008 this ancient language made its debut appearance in the European Parliament.

Violet Millar of Caeau Capel and a British Prime Minister
A regular visitor to Nefyn before and after the Second World War was Clement Attlee, the post-war British Prime Minister, who had married Violet Millar, one of the daughters from Caeau Capel, Rhodfa'r Môr, Nefyn.

A private hotel since the early 1930s, Caeau Capel had been built in the 1890s as a country house retreat for the family of Henry Edward Millar, a wealthy businessman from Hampstead, North London. On the 1901 census for London he is described as a commission merchant. There were eight children in the family, and the Millars employed five domestic servants in their Hampstead home, including Eliza Roberts, a 20 year old housemaid from Nefyn. Henry Edward Millar died in 1912 aged 55, and Caeau Capel was sold the following year.

Violet Millar and her twin sister were the youngest of the Millar children. In 1921, during a visit to Italy, Violet met Clement Attlee. He had served in the army during the Great War, he had been a lawyer and a university lecturer, but at the time of his introduction to Violet he had entered local politics to become the Mayor of Stepney in the East End of London.

Attlee and Violet Millar married in Hampstead on 10th January 1922. Later that year he entered Parliament as a Labour MP, and in due course he became leader of the party. During the Second World War he served as

Deputy Prime Minister in Churchill's wartime coalition government, and at the 1945 General Election he defeated Churchill overwhelmingly to become Prime Minister himself.

Although her old family holiday home in Nefyn had been sold many years previously, it seems that Violet retained a yearning to return to the place where she had spent so many happy times as a child. Therefore, for several years before, during and after the Second World War, Attlee and his family visited Nefyn each year for their summer holidays, even when he was Prime Minister. They stayed at Caeau Capel as well as Ty'n y Pwll and later Gorse Cliff. The Attlee family would arrive by car, complete with their pet dog and their cook. Apparently, when staying at Gorse Cliff, Attlee insisted on parking the cars on the main road for fear that the branches overhanging the narrow lane would scratch the paintwork on the vehicles.

In 2008 the *Guardian* published a series of photographs of political leaders on holiday. One of the images was a 1938 photograph of Attlee relaxing on Nefyn beach with his family. It depicts Attlee's wife sitting on the sand with her back resting against the side of a slipway. Attlee, dressed in a white shirt, sleeves rolled up, and wearing khaki shorts, is perching on the edge of the slipway beside her, while their two daughters, Janet and Felicity, are sitting on the sand, one on either side of their parents. In the background, beneath the cliff face, fishermen's huts and several small boats can be seen. Moreover, in the National Library of Wales there is a series of photographs of Attlee, his dog and the family cook standing outside the door of their Nefyn holiday accommodation.

When visiting Nefyn, Attlee loved to walk the cliff path between Nefyn and Morfa, and on one occasion he was almost knocked down by a group of young lads, who were cycling at breakneck speed along the path. Even after he became Prime Minister he could often be seen walking around the town in casual holiday attire, going in and out of the shops accompanied by his personal detectives. Local ladies remember him as an extremely polite gentleman who would step aside and hold the shop door open for them. Sometimes, when he was staying in the area, he could also be seen playing golf at the Nefyn Golf Club.

An Heroic Beach Rescue 1948

On the morning of Thursday July 22nd 1948 a local fisherman, Laurence Owen, went down to the beach which was already busy with holiday-makers. As he was preparing to go fishing he noticed something white floating in the water about 100 yards from the shore. He thought little of it until a woman, who was on holiday from Erdington in Birmingham, came running towards him, screaming that a canoe containing her three young children had capsized, plunging them all into the water. Immediately Laurence leapt into his boat and rowed as quickly as could to the upturned canoe, where he found one child desperately clinging to its side. But there was no sign of the two younger children. Immediately he dived to the sea bed where he found a toddler lying motionless. Grabbing hold of the child he rose to the surface, bundled the little lad into his rowing boat and dived again. This time he discovered a young girl lying limply in a bed of seaweed. Taking hold of her, he surfaced once more and pushed her into the boat. Then with the help of people in another boat he rescued the lad who was still holding onto the side of the canoe.

Having pulled all three children from the water, Laurence gave emergency first aid to the two lifeless children while the other boat towed his fishing boat to shore. Fortunately, before they reached the water's edge both of the unconscious children had begun to show signs of life, and Doctor Hughes Jones, who had been sent for, was waiting on the beach to take both children to hospital in Pwllheli.

Meanwhile Laurence Owen walked back home to change his clothes. On entering his house in Stryd y Llan his main concern was to dry out the packet of tobacco which had been in his pocket! This incident was narrated by Dr Brian Owen, Laurence's son, and the rescue was reported in the *Caernarfon and Denbigh Herald*. On September 14th 1948 Mr Laurence Owen was awarded a certificate from the Royal Humane Society for his courage and prompt actions in saving the lives of the three children.

The Rose Queen Festival and the Nefyn Carnival
During the post-war period an important annual event in Nefyn was the Rose Queen Festival, which was always held on August Bank Holiday Monday. On this important occasion a procession of decorated vehicles would wend its way through the streets of the town, led by the Nefyn Town Band. The specially decorated vehicles carried various tableaux, featuring children in fancy dress costumes, but the most important lorry carried the Nefyn Rose Queen, together with her ladies-in-waiting, her train bearers and flower girls. It was considered a great honour for a Nefyn girl to be chosen to be the Rose Queen.

Eventually the procession would make its way to the Madryn Hall for the all-important crowning ceremony, and the Hall was always packed to capacity. Afterwards the onlookers were able to enjoy a programme of dancing by local school children, and prizes were awarded to the fancy dress competition winners.

The Nefyn Carnival was one of the main events in the post-war calendar each year until it ceased in the 1980's. Subsequently it was replaced with an annual community festival but that also fell by the wayside.

On the May Bank Holiday 2009, the Nefyn carnival was resurrected under the guidance of a new organising committee, and the town centre was decorated with flags and bunting. The centre-piece of the Nefyn Carnival is still the procession of decorated floats, containing visiting queens, courts and princesses as well as participants on foot. At both carnivals in 2009 and 2010 the procession was led by the Dyffryn Nantlle Brass Band, since there is no longer a Nefyn Town Band. The procession eventually made its way to the Ysgol Nefyn Playing Field where a variety of attractions and entertainments had been laid on. In terms of the number of people attending and the amount of money raised, the 2010 Nefyn carnival was deemed to be a huge success, and there are plans to organise even more impressive carnivals in future years.

The Drowning of Two Nefyn Lads 1950

Approximately 18 months after the rescue of the three young Birmingham children in Nefyn Bay two Nefyn teenagers were tragically drowned.

It was New Year's Day 1950 when Hefin Hughes and Humphrey Davies set out from Nefyn beach in a sailing boat. Humphrey, who was the son of Captain Rowland Davies Fernlea, Stryd y Ffynnon, was home from the training school at South Shields on Tyneside where he was preparing for a career at sea. Hefin lived at London House, Pen y Bryn, where his parents kept the drapery store. He was an apprentice sailor, and he had already gained experience of sailing the oceans of the world.

When the two teenage friends set sail across Nefyn Bay that morning the weather was fine and there was no hint of the disaster that was to follow. During the afternoon a storm blew up with high winds and driving snow. Some time later, when the two lads failed to return, the alarm was raised and a search, involving both the Porth Dinllaen and Holyhead lifeboats, was organised. Several days later their upturned boat was discovered close to the Anglesey coast, but there was no sign of the two young sailors. It was clear that their boat had capsized in stormy weather and that both lads had been pitched into the sea and drowned. Their bodies were never recovered.

Following so soon after the loss of young Nefyn men during the Second World War, this was a tragedy which deeply affected the people of Nefyn. Both Hefin and Humphrey were Nefyn-born, they had grown up in the town and they were very well known in the area. It is extremely sad to think that these two lads were on the threshold of their careers at sea when their lives were so abruptly and cruelly cut short by the sea itself.

Nefyn and the Llŷn Pilgrimage of 1950

On Saint Peter's Day, 1950 there occurred an event which harked back across the centuries to the days when thousands of medieval pilgrims made their way from Saint Beuno's Church, Clynnog Fawr, down the peninsula and across to the holy island of Enlli. From the 6th century until the dissolution of the monasteries by Henry VIII Ynys Enlli had been home to communities of monks, and according to tradition 20,000 saints were buried on the island. Consequently Enlli was revered as a place of great sanctity, and during the Middle Ages large numbers of people undertook pilgrimages to the island.

On that day in 1950 hundreds of twentieth century pilgrims were intending to follow the route taken by the pilgrims of old, although on this occasion they were to complete the journey in a convoy of cars rather than on foot. It was a dull, drizzly day when the 20th century pilgrims gathered at the church of Saint Beuno at Clynnog. At certain places along the route 'hours' of prayers were to be said at specific times, in the manner of the ancient monastic tradition – Terce at 9.00 am, Sext at noon and None at 3.00 pm. Before the procession set off a Eucharist was held at Clynnog instead of the Terce of old.

Led by the Bishop of Bangor, and accompanied by a huge wooden cross, the long procession set out in hundreds of cars so that the journey could be completed in a single day. Of course, centuries ago it would have taken the medieval pilgrims travelling on foot, several days to complete the journey. As the long line of vehicles wended its way over the mountains near Tre'r Ceiri, it disappeared into a blanket of thick mist and low cloud.

At the little church of Saint Beuno in Pistyll, where a hospice had once existed, the 'pilgrim's bread' was shared amongst those taking part. At the old church of Saint Mary in Nefyn, next to the site of the ancient Celtic priory, the pilgrims paused to recite 'Sext' at noon. By 3.00 pm they had reached the historic church at Llangwnnadl for 'None'. Then the procession moved on to Aberdaron where the official souvenir booklet records that '3,000 pilgrims poured out of hundreds of cars'. Finally, with the bishop and the cross at its head, a huge column of people trailed down the hill on foot, over the old stone bridge and into the village.

From Saint Hywyn's church the crowds of people made their way to the edge of the sea, from where they looked across to the island. Unfortunately on that day gale force winds and rough seas rendered a crossing of the sound impossible. On the wave-swept beach the pilgrims sang hymns of praise and thanksgiving before laying up the cross to await a calmer day for the crossing. Undoubtedly this would not have been the first time that pilgrims had been forced to delay their crossing to await calmer conditions! The day ended at Saint Peter's Church in Pwllheli where the ancient Vespers found expression in Evensong. Here the bishop addressed the assembled pilgrims and gave a parting blessing.

A few days later, on 2nd August, when the sea was in calmer mood, a small party crossed the sound to Enlli to carry the cross to the ruins of the ancient monastery, thus ending the 20th century pilgrimage to the sacred isle. And so the Llŷn pilgrimage of 1950 was complete! This symbolic act by the people of Llŷn had forged a link across the centuries with the pilgrims and saints of old, and today it offers a poignant reminder of the important part that Llŷn has played in the history of Christianity in Wales.

The Last Great Herring Catch at Nefyn 1950
As has already been stated in the introduction, Nefyn was formerly one of the leading herring fishing ports in Wales, and Penwaig Nefyn (the herring caught in Nefyn Bay) were famous throughout Wales. However, for many years the shoals of herring had almost disappeared, and more recently local fishermen had tended to concentrate upon catching other types of fish.

Early in the morning on Sunday December 31st, 1950, Nefyn fisherman, Laurence Owen and his two sons, together with two fisherman friends, set off to go down to the beach. On the previous day they had set out several nets, some of which were in shallow-water while others had been secured in deeper water. They walked quietly through the town so that they would not draw attention to themselves, for Sunday was still considered to be a day of rest, and any kind of work on the Sabbath would have been frowned upon. It was a cold, frosty morning and, although the moon was shining, it was not a full moon which meant that the fish might have been persuaded to come nearer to the shore.

As the fishermen neared the bottom of the winding road which leads to the beach, they could see that the shallow-water nets, now lying on the sand, were full of herrings. One of the fishermen and the two lads began to remove the trapped fish from the nets, while Mr Owen and the other fisherman rowed out to the deep-water nets. They soon discovered that those nets were also full of fish, and they had to row back to the beach several times to carry the entire catch ashore. In total, the haul amounted to about 2500 herrings which filled 16 sacks, and they were fine fat specimens just like the ones that used to be caught at Nefyn many years ago.

On the following morning, news of the stupendous catch circulated around the town, and it was not long before people were calling at the fishermen's houses to purchase herrings. Practically everyone in the town bought herrings that day, and they were sold for one shilling per dozen. Since that day in 1950 other local fishermen have caught herrings in the bay, but never again have their catches compared with the haul of December 1950, which was almost certainly the last great herring catch at Porth Nefyn. This story was told by Dr Brian Owen who, as a young child, helped his father, Lawrence, to remove the fish from the nets.

A Young Nefyn Man is Drowned at Bodeilias 1952

Another local drowning tragedy occurred in 1952 when the body of a 23 year old Nefyn man, John Charles Evans, was found lying face down in the dock at Bodeilias Point. This was the dock where coastal vessels had once loaded up with granite from the Bodeilias Quarry, but by 1950 both the quarry and the dock had ceased to operate many years previously.

John Charles was the son of Mr & Mrs Charles Evans, of Number 11 Nant y Felin. At about 11 am on the morning of Saturday 12th July Gwilym Roberts of Wern Farm was working in a hay field called Cae Mawr when John Charles walked through the field accompanied by two sheep dogs. The young man, who appeared to be in very good spirits, said that he was going to the beach to collect some wood which he had hidden there.

On that same evening Rowland Hallam, a farmer of Minffordd Farm, Pistyll, decided to go fishing at Penrhyn Bodeilias. Soon after arriving he spotted a brown shoe lying on the rocks above the beach, but he thought nothing of it until he noticed a body floating face down in the water in the corner of the Bodeilias dock. Immediately he hurried away to notify PC Jones who returned with him to the disused dock.

Subsequently an inquest was held at Bryn Beryl Hospital. It was concluded that John Charles must have been clambering on the rocks above the dock when he slipped and fell, striking his head on the stonework. Sadly, this must have caused him to lose consciousness before toppling into the dock where he drowned. A verdict of 'Accidental Death' was recorded on the young man.[4]

A Library for Nefyn 1955

Nefyn did not possess a public library until the middle of the 20th century, although certain book-lending facilities did exist in the town several years earlier than that.

The passing of the 1870 Education Act, and the provision of schooling for every 5-13 year old at local Board schools, gradually created a wider reading public and the need for a supply of readily available books. Eventually, local towns recognised this need, and they began to open book-lending facilities for the benefit of their communities. Between 1870 and 1910 nine Caernarfonshire towns and parishes, including Cricieth (1904) and Porthmadog (1910) set up their own independent lending libraries. But, as yet, Nefyn had no such resource.

Following the passing of the Public Libraries Act in 1919 Caernarfonshire Education Committee, with the backing of the Carnegie Trust, agreed to implement a scheme by which a large collection of books would be housed centrally in Caernarfon so that they could be sent out to schools throughout the county. These books would then be made available to teachers and children, as well as to adults and youngsters who had already left school. Thus Caernarfonshire schools were to act as lending libraries, thereby ensuring that the inhabitants of every parish in the county had access to books which could be borrowed.

The supply of books in each school was changed at regular intervals. J. Ifor Davies recalls 'the boxfuls of County Library books which reached the school at regular intervals throughout the year' and which the children 'dutifully queued up to borrow.' Among the books most in demand were the acknowledged classics, mainly in English. It was reported by Heads of schools in 1924 that the scheme was encouraging the habit of reading, not only amongst the pupils in school but also amongst the youngsters who had already left. However, the demand for books was much greater in the slate quarrying areas of the county than in other parts, especially Llŷn and South Caernarfonshire.

J. Ifor Davies also mentions a small private lending library located at No 1 Marine Terrace, where two sisters, Miss Maggie Jones and Miss Jane Jones, had accumulated a large stock of books which they were happy to lend out to anyone who knocked on their door. But, as young children, John Ifor and his friends did not find most of the available reading material either exciting or easy to cope with.

A huge step forward occurred in the early 1950's when Caernarfonshire County Council began to establish part-time branch lending libraries, and Nefyn obtained its own purpose-built local authority lending library in 1955.

One of the problems for local librarians had always been the lack of new reading material published in Welsh. A major step forward in this regard was taken in 1960 when the 'Welsh Books Council' was set up to promote the publication of Welsh language books. As a result of this initiative there has been a noticeable change in the number of Welsh books being borrowed. According to a survey, in the mid 1950's only one Welsh language book was borrowed for every 16 books printed in English. By 1967-8 the proportion was one Welsh book for every four English books, and the current proportion is undoubtedly much more heavily weighted in favour of Welsh-language reading material.

Today the Nefyn Library also has several computers with internet access available for use, and it is possible to borrow audio books and DVDs. In 2010 Gwynedd Council secured a Welsh Assembly grant to refurbish and improve the facilities in the Nefyn library. These improvements have resulted in a noticeable increase in the use of the library's facilities, especially by children.

Nefyn Sailing Club 1957
As previously mentioned, there are references to a regatta in Nefyn before the beginning of the 20th century. In July 1893 local newspapers reported a disaster when two men drowned at the Nefyn Regatta, their boat having capsized in the bay. In the period between the two world wars the Nefyn Regatta, which was always held in August, was one of the main events each year. There were yacht races in the morning, followed in the afternoon by rowing and swimming contests in the bay, and all manner races and competitions on the beach. On that day every house along the Morfa Road would have a flag flying from a flagpole, and there would be great excitement as the crowds lined the cliff top to watch the yachts setting off across the bay, each attempting to gain an advantage over its rivals. The Second World War put an end to the traditional Nefyn Regatta.

The present sailing club, which has a club house on the beach at Porth Nefyn, was founded in 1957, and it is run mainly by visitors. Each year during the month of August there is a full programme of racing for all types of boats and all kinds of sailors. A number of cups are competed for, and all races are sailed on handicap under RYA rules. The sailing club also organises a programme of social events throughout the month of August.

Professor Herbert Rees Wilson
A particularly noteworthy son of Nefyn is Professor Herbert Wilson, a scientist and a member of one of the research teams which worked on the structure of DNA in the early 1950s.

He was related to the Rees family of Pistyll Farm, as well as the Thomas family of Tŷ Mawr Farm, Pistyll. His paternal great grandfather, Robert Morris Wilson who kept the Prince of Wales Vaults in Stryd Moreia, married Jane Rees of Pistyll Farm. His paternal grandfather, Thomas Rees Wilson, a quarryman living in Stryd y Ffynnon, married Mary Thomas, the daughter of Herbert Thomas of Tŷ Mawr Farm – hence Professor Wilson's Christian name, Herbert.

Like many Nefyn children, Herbert Wilson was born into a family of seamen. His father was Captain Robert Morris Wilson of Derlwyn, while his uncles were Captain Thomas Rees Wilson, who survived both world wars at sea, and Herbert Rees Wilson, a ship's steward who died of cholera in Russia at the age of 20. His great uncle was Captain William Wilson, who survived the sinking of the *Powys Castle* near Cape Horn in 1903.

Herbert Wilson was educated at the Nefyn school, the Pwllheli County School and the University College of Wales Bangor, where he graduated with a first class degree in physics. As a PhD student he worked on the construction of metals, but it was the field of biophysics that appealed to him most of all. In 1952 he joined a project at King's College London, to carry out research into DNA.

In April 1953 three papers were published simultaneously in the scientific journal, 'Nature', to announce the discovery of the double helix structure of DNA, one of the most significant scientific discoveries of the 20th century. One paper was presented by Francis Crick and James Watson (from the Cavendish Laboratory at Cambridge University), another was written by Rosalind Franklin (from King's College London), and the third was published by Maurice Wilkins's group (also based at King's College), of which Herbert Wilson was a member.

This ground-breaking work resulted in Crick, Watson and Wilkins being jointly awarded the 1962 Nobel Prize for Physiology. Franklin's contribution was not recognised in the award because she had died in 1958 at the age of 37 and Nobel Prizes cannot be awarded posthumously. Controversially, the extremely important contributions made by Herbert Wilson and the other junior members of the King's College teams were not recognised in the Stockholm award.

Doctor Wilson continued with his work at King's College until 1957. Subsequently he was appointed Lecturer in Physics at Queen's College, Dundee, and then at the Universities of Saint Andrews and Dundee. In 1962 he was appointed Visiting Research Associate at the Children's Cancer Research Foundation in Boston, Massachusetts, and in 1963 he became Professor of Physics at Stirling University.

In 2005 he was awarded an honorary doctorate in Science from the University of Wales and a Fellowship from his former college at Bangor. Among other honours bestowed upon him were his election to the Fellowship of the Royal Society of Edinburgh and the Rodman Medal for his X-ray images of DNA. In 2004 he was also honoured at the National Eisteddfod of Wales when he was admitted to the Gorsedd of Bards under the name of 'Herbert Wyddonydd' (Herbert Scientist). Sadly, four years later, in May 2008, Professor Wilson died. He is survived by his wife, Beti (a Nefyn girl) and their two daughters.

Apparently Herbert and Beti both took part in a school play at Ysgol Nefyn when they were six years old, and in one scene Beti had to give Herbert a treacle sandwich. A former classmate, Glyn O. Phillips, has suggested that it 'must have been a very special sandwich because after that he held onto Beti Turner very tightly, and she fed and supported him from that time onwards.'[5]

The importance of the DNA research in which Herbert Wilson and the others were involved cannot be over-emphasised, for it has resulted in a great many extremely important advances. It has made possible genetic engineering in plants and animals, it has facilitated massive improvements in forensic science, and it has resulted in huge advances in medical research. Without the earlier pioneering work into DNA, research and treatments using stem cells would not be possible. Although the use of stem cells is still in its infancy it is predicted that, in future, such techniques will have the potential to cure a wide range of debilitating and life-threatening human conditions, including Parkinson's Disease, Multiple Sclerosis, Cystic Fibrosis and spinal chord injuries.

Very recently, in December 2009, it was reported that a young Australian Multiple Sclerosis sufferer, who was wheelchair-bound, has received stem cell treatment, as a result of which his condition has improved to such an extent that he is now able to walk again.[6] During 2011 it was also reported that scientists at Edinburgh University had succeeded in creating human kidneys from stem cells, an advance which has far-reaching implications in the future for patients requiring kidney transplants. Therefore it can be stated unequivocally that the pioneering work of Herbert Wilson, and the others who worked on the structure of DNA sixty years ago, has been of inestimable benefit in a variety of ways to humankind throughout the entire world.

A plaque, mounted on the front of the Strand Campus of King's College, London, commemorates the achievement of King's College researchers. It reads:

> Near this site Rosalind Franklin, Maurice Wilkins, Raymond Gosling, Alexander Stokes and Herbert Wilson performed experiments that led to the discovery of the structure of DNA. This work revolutionised our understanding of the chemistry behind life itself.

The Nefyn Street-Naming Rumpus of the 1960s
In 1963 the Ministry of Transport issued a directive to all Councils in England and Wales that they should assess whether their street name plates were adequate in helping people to find the addresses for which they were searching. But in Nefyn there never had been any street name plates and so, in respect of this little town, the Council ('Lleyn Rural District Council' at the time) had to start from scratch.

This entire exercise sparked off a heated debate among the townsfolk concerning the wording that should appear on those new name plates. The question was this – should they be in Welsh alone or should they be in English as well as Welsh, largely for the benefit of English visitors? There were some who advocated Welsh-only name plates while others favoured bilingual signs. Naturally, in every day speech local Nefyn folk had always referred to the streets by their Welsh names, Stryd y Ffynnon, Stryd Fawr, Stryd y Plas, etc. However, over the years, on large scale OS maps, on picture post cards and on official documents, Nefyn streets had always been referred to by their English equivalent names, Well Street, High Street, Palace Street etc. The problem was further complicated by the fact that, for certain local road names, there were no appropriate English equivalents, as in the case of Tai Lôn and Y Maes.

The debate raged on, and the arguments hit the headlines in the local press. In the end, common sense prevailed when it was decided that Nefyn streets should bear only the Welsh names which had been used by local inhabitants for generations. And as for the visitors, they cope with Stryd y Ffynnon, Stryd Fawr and Stryd y Plas just as they cope with French, Spanish and German street names when they visit the continent of Europe!

Nefyn and the 1969 Investiture
The actual investiture of Prince Charles did not take place at Caernarfon Castle until 1st July 1969, although the Letters Patent by which he had been granted the title 'Prince of Wales' were dated 26th July 1958. The idea of investing the heir to the throne as 'Prince of Wales' dates back to 1301 when Edward I of England gave the title to his son, Prince Edward, who later became Edward II.

Across Wales views about the investiture, and all that it stood for, were polarised. Some people were excited at the prospect of this colourful occasion, and large crowds gathered in Caernarfon to witness the event which was seen on television across Britain and throughout the entire world. But there were other Welsh people who opposed it passionately. For them the ceremony at Caernarfon was symbolic of the defeat of the last native

Prince of Wales by Edward I of England, and the subjugation of the Welsh nation.

There were threats of violence on the day of the investiture, security for the occasion was tight and two ardent opponents of the event were accidentally blown up by their own bomb as they sought to derail the train on which they believed the royal party would be travelling. There were strong feelings about the event in Nefyn, too. A huge slogan painted across the front of the Midland Bank read 'DIM SAIS YN DYWYSOG CYMRU' (*No Englishman is Prince of Wales*).

R. Gerallt Jones

R. Gerallt Jones, Welsh educationalist, poet, novelist and literary critic, was the son of a High Church Anglican clergyman. He was born in 1934 at his grandmother's home, half way between Nefyn and Morfa Nefyn. It was here that Gerallt spent much of his childhood, before and during the Second World War. A monoglot Welsh speaker until the age of 10, Gerallt attended the schools at Dinas and Morfa Nefyn. After a time his father moved him to a boarding preparatory school near Shrewsbury, and finally to a minor English public school, Denstone College in Staffordshire, although his heart remained firmly in his native Llŷn. Subsequently he wrote, 'Wales for me was a hearth, a home, a wonderful world, hidden, separate from the world of school, a proud possession of my own, a secret room that my English friends knew nothing about.'

His higher education was obtained at the University College of Wales, Bangor, where he read English before going on to write an MA thesis on the work of the poet Robert Graves.

He began his career as a schoolteacher in Amlwch, Angelsey, before being appointed lecturer in the Education Department at the University College of Wales, Aberystwyth. After a spell as principal of a teachers' training college in Jamaica, he returned to Wales to become the warden of Llandovery College, the only Welsh public school. In 1989 he was appointed warden of Greynog Hall, the University of Wales residential study centre in Powys. Here he remained until his retirement in 1995.

He served as a lay reader and member of the Governing Body of the Church in Wales, and he was a member of several other important bodies – the Broadcasting Council for Wales, the Welsh Arts Council, the Court of the University of Wales Aberystwyth, the Welsh National Film and Video Archive, and the Board of Governors of S4C.

R. Gerallt Jones was remarkably versatile in his writing. He published five volumes of poetry in Welsh and one in English; he published literary criticism in both languages; he was a regular contributor to Welsh periodicals between 1987 and 1992; he penned five novels in Welsh, two of which won the Prose Medal at the National Eisteddfod of Wales in 1977 and 1979; his collection of seven short stories about a lad growing up in Llŷn during the Second World War was adapted for television on S4C, and one of those stories 'The Evacuees' was screened at the London Film Festival.

R. Gerallt Jones died in January 1999, before he was able to fulfil his ambition of returning to live in Llŷn. He is survived by his wife and their three children. His book, *A Place in the Mind*, is a fascinating and beautifully written account of the Llŷn of his boyhood during the late 1930s and 1940s. It was published by his wife in 2004, five years after her husband's death.

The Fire on Garn Boduan 1979

One hot summer's day in July 1979 a huge forest fire broke out in a Forestry Commission plantation on the side of Garn Boduan. It was a fire which could be seen from many miles away and, as the *Caernarfon and Denbigh Herald* records, it was 'one of the most serious outbreaks of fire in the area for many years.'[7] The alarm was raised at about 4.00 pm on Wednesday 25th July. Fire appliances rushed to the Garn from Nefyn, Pwllheli, Abersoch and Porthmadog, and the firemen were assisted by Forestry Commission workmen and local volunteers.

The fire fighters toiled for hours to bring the fire under control but there were several difficulties. Since the Garn is fairly remote the water had to be pumped to the scene from a hydrant in Boduan, nearly a mile away, and several miles of hose pipe were deployed in this operation. A heavy ground mist, which eventually enveloped the area, made it difficult for the firemen to spot fresh outbreaks of fire along the rocky slopes. In due course fire appliances from Caernarfon and Blaenau Ffestiniog arrived to relieve some of the crews already there.

When, on the evening of Monday 30th July, torrential rain finally arrived, the resulting downpour ensured that there would be no further outbreaks of fire. However, by this time the side of the Garn had been burning and smouldering for six days.

Altogether, during that week, 10,000 trees had been destroyed on the 1000 feet high mountain, and several acres of unplanted ground were also burnt.[8] More than 30 years after the event it is still possible to see the after-effects of that fire. As you drive along the road from the Bryncynan Inn towards Nefyn you cannot help noticing that the side of the Garn facing you is totally devoid of trees apart from a number of stark upstanding tree trunks.

RNLI Medals for Porth Dinllaen Lifeboatmen
Three bronze medals and one silver medal have been awarded to members of the Porth Dinllaen lifeboat crew since the Second World War.

On 8th August 1951, on a particularly dark night and in extremely rough seas, the lifeboat was launched at 10.10 pm to search for a yacht which was long overdue. Eventually the missing yacht was spotted at anchor close to the rocky shore near Porth Oer. With the wind reaching gale force, and the sea battering both the lifeboat and the yacht, Second Coxswain William Dop, with enormous skill, managed to negotiate his way between the rocks to get alongside the yacht so that its three crew members could be rescued. Finally, he skilfully manoeuvred the lifeboat stern first into deeper water before returning to station at 5.30 am. For his gallantry and superb seamanship William Dop was awarded the RNLI Silver Medal.

On the night of September 20th 1974 off-duty Coxswain Griffith Jones went to the lifeboat station with his 14 year old son, Eric, because the lifeboat was being launched. A dinghy had capsized in rough seas off Porth Dinllaen. In the headlights of a coastguard vehicle young Eric spotted one of the men from the dinghy clinging to a rock about 400 yards from the boathouse. Coxswain Jones and his son launched the station's boarding boat, and in a 12 foot swell made their way between the rocks to rescue the man who was in shock and utterly exhausted. For his great skill and tremendous courage Griffith Jones was awarded an RNLI bronze medal, while his son was presented with an inscribed wrist watch.

Another RNLI medal was awarded for an outstanding rescue on the night of August 31st 1976 when two lads were trapped on the cliffs at Porth Nant, north east of Nefyn. Since it was impossible to take the lifeboat close to the shore on account of the rough seas and dangerous rocks, Second Coxswain John Scott, using a smaller boarding boat, landed Lifeboatman Glyn Roberts at the foot of the cliffs. One of the boys was still trapped 80 feet above the shoreline, so Lifeboatman Roberts removed his sea boots and socks before climbing the almost sheer cliff face, to rescue the terrified lad. For his gallantry and disregard for his own personal safety, Lifeboatman Glyn Roberts was awarded a bronze medal by the RNLI. He also received an award for the most outstanding RNLI life-saving rescue of 1976.

On the afternoon of 25th April 1981 news reached the lifeboat station that a dinghy had capsized and two persons were in the water. When the lifeboat reached the scene one man was on top of the upturned dinghy and the other was floundering in the sea. The conditions were horrendous with 15 foot waves breaking over the lifeboat and crashing into the wheelhouse. Several attempts were made to manoeuvre the lifeboat close to the two men, and eventually both were rescued and airlifted to hospital in Bangor suffering from exposure. The sea was so hostile that it was impossible to return the lifeboat to its station, and so the crew had to be evacuated by helicopter. Acting Coxswain Michael Masserelli was awarded an RNLI Bronze Medal for his outstanding seamanship and great courage in carrying out this rescue.

Not all lifeboat rescues turn out to be difficult and dangerous, but the ones described briefly above serve to remind us that, on occasions, the volunteer crews of our lifeboat service are required to go to sea in terrifying conditions, thus putting their own safety in jeopardy whilst attempting to save the lives of others.

The Burning of a Nefyn Holiday Home 1979

As the people of Nefyn awoke on the morning of December 13th 1979 they knew nothing of the previous night's events. A holiday home on Mynydd Nefyn, called Tyddyn Gwêr, had been set on fire and completely destroyed. Another holiday home, Sŵn y Môr at Llanbedrog, had also been destroyed, in addition two holiday houses at Pennal near Machynlleth and another two at Llanrhian in Pembrokeshire. The fire at Tyddyn Gwêr was first spotted by a neighbour at three o'clock in the early hours of that Thursday morning, and the alarm was raised. Fire engines from Nefyn and Pwllheli raced to the mountain, but by the time they arrived the cottage was completely gutted.[9]

Clearly those arson attacks across Wales were part of a carefully planned and co-ordinated campaign, which was later attributed to a shadowy movement known as Meibion Glyndŵr (*the Sons of Glyndŵr*). Those attacks constituted the forerunner of a concerted campaign which also involved fire-bombing holiday-makers' cars and yachts. The campaign even spread into England where estate agents who sold Welsh properties were targeted in a similar manner.

Despite the work of the forensic experts who sifted through the ruins of Tyddyn Gwêr and, in spite of extensive enquiries by local police and a substantial reward for information, the arsonists were never apprehended, and to this day the identity of those who took action in the name of Meibion Glyndŵr remains an unsolved mystery.

The Opening of the Nefyn Maritime Museum 1979

In 1979 the Nefyn Maritime Museum was established in the old Saint Mary's Church, the last service having been held there on Thursday 8th September, 1978.

The church building itself is an historic one, having been erected in 1825-7 on the site of earlier churches, for there has probably been a place of worship on this site since the 6th century. The present building, standing in its ancient raised churchyard, is characterised by its tall slender tower which is surmounted by a weather vane in the shape of a sailing ship – a constant reminder of Nefyn's rich maritime past. Inside the church there is a medieval font and a grave stone which bears an inscription to the memory of centagenarian Elin Wyn Saython, the wife of John Parry of Nefyn 1679. The ancient churchyard contains the interesting graves of scores of local mariners and master mariners.

The museum itself houses a wealth of artefacts, photographs, paintings, models and documents relating to the local ship building industry, the Nefyn herring fishing, coasting vessels and oceanic sailing as well as everyday life in Nefyn from the end of the 19th century. This body of material, which has been gathered together at the museum with the help of local residents and the Gwynedd Archives Service, is hugely impressive and extremely interesting.

After receiving visitors every summer for 23 years, the museum was forced to close its doors in the year 2000, owing to the unsatisfactory condition of the building, especially the roof which was considered unsafe. A considerable sum of money would be needed to restore the building so that the museum could reopen. Initially, certain efforts were made to raise funds, and plans for the work to be carried out were drawn up, but it all came to nothing. In 2007 a new committee was formed and a grant of money was obtained to carry out some emergency repairs. Subsequently, the museum opened again for five days during the month of August. It is understood that substantial additional funding has now been secured, and that there are plans to reopen the museum and expand its scope so that it will include material which covers the maritime history and life of people throughout the entire peninsula.

It is to be hoped that the refurbishment of the building will be carried out in the near future, so that the museum will be able to open again for longer periods each summer. The Nefyn Maritime Museum must not to be allowed to disappear into oblivion, for it provides a fascinating visual record of the area's daily life and seafaring heritage!

John Ifor Davies

John Ifor Davies, linguist, headmaster and writer on local maritime history, was born and bred in Nefyn. Born in 1908, he was the son of Captain William and Mrs Grace Davies, Craig y Môr. Captain Davies spent most of his career sailing on the ships which belonged to Robert Thomas & Company of Cricieth and Liverpool.

Young John Ifor spent the first four years of his life at sea with his parents and his elder sister aboard the three-masted barque *Gwydir Castle*, of which his father was the master. At that time Captains' wives, together with their young children, often accompanied their husbands on board their ships. Indeed, the children of some ships' captains were actually born on board ship. When John Ifor's sister was old enough to go to school Mrs Davies and her children were forced to give up their roving way of life at sea. Having attained school age, John Ifor himself attended Nefyn Council School, before passing the scholarship to go to Pwllheli County School.

In 1926 Captain Davies, John Ifor's father, was taken seriously ill during his last voyage before retirement. His ship, the *Monkbarns*, put into harbour in Rio de Janeiro and the captain was taken to hospital where he died shortly afterwards. On hearing the distressing news of her husband's sudden death, Mrs Davies, who had been the head teacher of the Nefyn Board School prior to her marriage, informed her two sons that under no circumstances would they be pursuing a career in the Merchant Navy. John Ifor later admitted that this piece of news did not come as a bitter disappointment to him. Instead he decided to follow in the footsteps of his mother and become a teacher. He gained a place at the University College of Wales Bangor, where he graduated with a first class honours degree in French and English. He went on to gain an MA with distinction for his researches into 'The French Influences on Swinburne'. He also spent time at the Universities of Strasbourg and Paris.

His first teaching post in 1932 was that of Senior French Master at the West Monmouth School, Pontypool. During the war he joined the Royal Air Force Volunteer Reserve before becoming the headmaster of Caernarfon County School in 1944. During the 1960's, with the advent of comprehensive education, his grammar school was reorganised into a comprehensive school with a new name, Ysgol Gyfun Syr Hugh Owen. Although this was a change which he appeared to regret, he remained as head of the school until his retirement in December 1973.

Despite the fact that Ifor Davies had turned his back upon a career at sea to become a teacher, it is clear that he retained an intense interest in maritime and local history. In 1987 he was prompted to write 'Growing Up Among Sailors', an excellent book in which he relives, not only his early years on board his father's sailing ship, but also his later childhood experiences of life within the maritime community of Nefyn before and after the Great War.

Between 1977 and 1989 he contributed several articles to Cymru a'r Môr

(Maritime Wales) and in 1989 he published the history of Caernarfon County School. His book, 'Growing Up Among Sailors', and his articles in Cymru a'r Môr provide valuable resources for local and maritime historians wishing to research Nefyn's past.

The Llŷn Earthquake of 1984

On 19th July 1984 there occurred a huge earthquake in Gwynedd with its epicentre between Nefyn and Llithfaen. The British Geological Survey states that 'of those British earthquakes with onshore epicentres, this event is one of the largest, if not the largest of those for which magnitude can be determined or estimated.' The magnitude of this earthquake was between 5 and 5.5 on the scale, and its 'felt area' covered approximately 240,000 square kilometres, encompassing all of Wales, most of England, the east coast of Ireland and part of southern Scotland. The earthquake occurred at a depth of 22 kilometres and was followed by many aftershocks.

In thê immediate area of northern Llŷn damage was surprisingly slight – some plaster damage in houses, a few fallen chimneys, several collapsed field walls and the loss of electricity supplies across the peninsula. Professor Geoffrey King of Cambridge University commented, 'Had this not been a rural area with strong Welsh stone buildings, this earthquake could have been devastating.'[10] Further afield there was damage to old properties in Liverpool, a chimney fell in London and a bungalow was severely damaged in Shropshire.

There are records of previous earthquakes in Llŷn during the 20th century. Records kept by the Earthquake Documentation and Research Centre show that there was an earthquake near Nefyn on 13th January 1932. Its epicentre was at Boduan where the only damage was a boiling kettle which fell off the hob in a cottage. On 12th December 1940 another Llŷn earthquake occurred. On this occasion, John Thomas of Nefyn suffered a heart attack 'owing to the extreme loudness of the noise', and he died the following day.[11] At the same time *The Cambrian News* recorded another fatality in Cricieth where an elderly woman, Mrs Williams, was woken by the noise of the earthquake. In a state of great agitation she attempted to descend to the ground floor but fell down the stairs and died as a result of her fall.

The Twinning of Nefyn with Porth Madryn 1998

September 1998 saw the twinning of Nefyn (population of just over 2,000) with the Patagonian city of Porth Madryn (called Puerto Madryn in Argentina), a city of roughly 70,000 people. A delegation of people from

Nefyn travelled to Porth Madryn for the twinning ceremony, and people from Porth Madryn visited Nefyn.

To many people it might seem strange that a very small, quiet town on the northern coast of the Llŷn peninsula has been twinned with a bustling city of 70,000 people in far off South America. However, there are very sound reasons for such a twinning, and the connection between the two places lies in the name 'Madryn'. Porth Madryn was so named after Madryn Castle, the Jones Parry family estate which is situated about three miles from Nefyn. For many centuries the Madryn Estate was an important landowner in Nefyn and indeed throughout Llŷn. The house itself was destroyed by fire and pulled down in the 1960s, so that only an incomplete late medieval gatehouse now remains. The site is currently occupied by a caravan and chalet park.

The connection between Madryn and Patagonia goes back to 1862 when Captain Love Jones Parry of Madryn Castle travelled to Argentina. There he joined up with Lewis Jones, a Caernarfon-born printer, who had gone out to investigate the possibility of establishing a Welsh community in that country. Their main purpose was to acquire some land where a Welsh settlement could be founded and where the Welsh language and culture could be preserved indefinitely. For many years The Revd Michael D. Jones, a Nonconformist minister and principal of Bala College, had been of the opinion that Wales was in danger of losing its native tongue and heritage. He believed that if the Welsh national character and language were to survive and flourish, free from English influence, then strong well-organised Welsh-speaking communities must be established abroad.

There had already been preliminary discussions with the Government of Argentina, and after holding further talks with the Argentinean Interior Minister in Buenos Aires, Love Jones Parry and Lewis Jones secured an offer of land in Patagonia. The two men travelled south in the small ship *Candelaria* so that they could view the land which they had recently abeen granted. As they neared the end of their journey a violent storm blew up and their ship was forced ashore into a bay on the Patagonian coast. They decided to call that place Porth Madryn after Love Jones Parry's ancestral home. When Love Jones Parry and Lewis Jones returned to Wales they brought back favourable reports about the land which they had secured. A booklet, entitled 'Y Wladfa' (the homeland), was produced for people who were thinking of emigrating to take up the challenge of building a new Welsh society in South America.

In May 1865 153 Welsh folk set out from the port of Liverpool in an old tea clipper, the *Mimosa*, bound for Patagonia. The passenger list records that they came from all parts of North and South Wales, but there are no entries relating to Nefyn folk. Those early emigrants were true pioneers, for the land which they had been granted was not rich and fertile as they had been led to believe. The Chubut Valley, where the Welsh settlers finally settled, was very dry and rather infertile. They were forced to endure a great deal of hardship, including several disasters, as they sought to create a suitable homeland there.

Furthermore, over the years, the Welsh in Patagonia have had a struggle to preserve their language and Welsh way of life in a predominantly Spanish-speaking country. In 1930, when Jose Felix Uriburu, a right wing politician, seized power in Argentina he banned the use of Welsh in public, causing it to become an underground language. Once again, when the military junta of General Galtieri seized power in 1981, the government attempted to suppress the Welsh language, and Welsh-speaking parents were even forbidden to give their children Welsh Christian names. However, since then, a number of initiatives have been introduced to promote the Welsh language, and it is blossoming again in Y Wladfa.

Today there are estimated to be about 20,000 people of Welsh ancestry living in Porth Madryn and in other townships within the region, including about 5000 Welsh speakers and hundreds more who are learning Welsh. The language has made pleasing progress in the Chubut province since the introduction of the Welsh Language Project in 1997. Apart from Nefyn's twinning arrangement with Porth Madryn there are strong cultural links between Wales and Y Wladfa via Cymdeithas Cymru-Ariannin (*Wales-Argentina Society*). Welsh Patagonians regularly come to Wales to attend the National Eisteddfod and Welsh-speakers from Wales frequently go to Patagonia on teacher and student exchanges, on holiday or to undertake some kind of work.

Nefyn's twinning arrangement with Porth Madryn is commemorated on the approach roads to Nefyn in the form of large signs which are written in both Welsh and Spanish. In Porth Madryn the twinning arrangement is celebrated by inscriptions on two pieces of Welsh stone which are attached to a wall inside the town hall. Those two stone tablets, a substantial piece of granite from Madryn Castle and a smaller plaque of Welsh slate, were both selected by a former mayor of Porth Madryn during his visit to Llŷn. Apparently he carried them all the way back to Patagonia in his hand luggage!

A Fatal Landslide at Nefyn 2001

A geological feature at Nefyn which has caused certain problems is the composition of the coastline in Nefyn Bay. The two headlands, Penrhyn

Bodeilias and Penrhyn Nefyn are composed of a hard-wearing, course-grained, granite-type rock, but the arc of cliffs between those two headlands consists of layers of boulder clay, silt, gravel, stones and sand. These are the materials left behind by the ice sheets and glaciers as they retreated at the end of the last Ice Age.

These layers of glacial sediment can become unsafe in very wet weather and, following prolonged periods of rainfall, several landslides have occurred along the bay. When large amounts of rainwater permeate through the layers of sediment to saturate them, they become sodden and prone to break away from the cliff face. When that happens, large amounts of clay and mud slide downwards towards the beach. For many years there have been such landslides along these cliffs, as evidenced by old postcards.

A serious landslide occurred here on 3rd January 2001 when sadly a local woman was killed. The period from August 2000 to February 2001 was one of the wettest on record, with the rainfall in Llŷn one and a half times greater than the average. On that particular morning Mr and Mrs Race from Tudweiliog were sitting in their car in one of the parking spaces at the bottom of Lôn Gam. As they sat there, overlooking the sea, a huge amount of soil and debris suddenly broke away from the cliff side, slid downwards, spilled across the road, and engulfed their car as well as several other vehicles which were unoccupied. The car containing Mr and Mrs Race was pushed forward until it was teetering on the edge of the road with a sheer drop to the beach below. With a mass of material surrounding them the couple were unable to open their car doors to escape. Minutes after the first landslide, there occurred a second one, which sent their car and another unoccupied vehicle plunging over the edge onto the beach 25 feet below. Tragically, Mrs Race was thrown from the car and killed.

With the tide coming in, rescuers worked frantically to free Mr Race from his vehicle so that he could be rushed to hospital in Bangor. Because it was feared that other people may have been trapped beneath the mass of debris, thermal imaging equipment and mechanical diggers were brought in. Fortunately no other casualties were found although seven parked vehicles had been engulfed by the landslip on that day, and several people were fortunate not to have been swept away by the mass of mud.

On that day the rescue operation involved a helicopter from RAF Valley, members of the local cliff rescue service, firefighters, paramedics, North Wales Police, search dogs and the Porth Dinllaen lifeboat. News items describing this disaster appeared in the local and national press, while pictures of the scene were beamed around the country on numerous television news bulletins.

Within a short period of time the beach road and the cliff path had been closed, and several months later engineering works were carried out on the cliff face above Lôn Gam to stabilise it and make it safe, while the path on top of the cliff was diverted away from the cliff edge. Thanks to this remedial work there is every chance that there will be no further landslips above Lôn Gam.

However, in November 2009, following another period of sustained and intense rainfall, there was another landslip at the Penrhyn Nefyn end of the bay, near the breakwater. This time a large amount of debris broke away and slid down the cliff face, completely demolishing two beach chalets and destroying the end of a third hut. Fortunately no one was injured on that occasion.

If one walks along the beach towards Bodeilias Point one can see evidence of numerous minor landslips with large hollows scooped out of the cliff face and clumps of debris lying on the beach below.

Graffiti Daubing at Nefyn 2002
During the night of Sunday 21st /Monday 22nd April 2002 several anti-English slogans were daubed in white paint on a number of walls and buildings within the town, including private houses, shops and public buildings such as the disused Madryn Hall. Altogether about a dozen sites were targeted. Some of the graffiti was daubed in English, while other slogans were painted in Welsh. No one claimed responsibility, but the properties of both English and Welsh people were affected. Sites seemed to have been selected simply because they were situated in prominent positions where they would be clearly visible. Among the slogans left behind were 'I'r Gad' (*to battle*) and the initials 'MG' (Meibion Glyndŵr), which caused considerable anxiety amongst many members of the local community who blamed the graffiti on people from outside the town. These slogans were clearly intended to highlight the dangers to the Welshness of the area posed by the incursion of English influences.

Many people were concerned about the potential negative effects of those slogans. Councillor Bob Trenholme said, 'Local people are very angry about this. Of course we need to protect the Welsh language and culture, but this is not the way to do it.'[12] The Llŷn Tourist Association also expressed concern. Its marketing officer and events organiser stated, 'We need to keep young people in the area, and that depends on employment. Tourism therefore has a major contribution to make. These slogans cannot be beneficial.'[13] Since visitors are important to the economy of Nefyn, especially during the summer season, there was also a great deal of anxiety amongst the owners of local businesses.

Doctor Robyn Léwis

Another well-known son of Nefyn is Doctor Robyn Léwis, solicitor, barrister, author, Emeritus Archdruid of Wales and passionate defender of the Welsh language and culture.

Despite being born in Llangollen, Doctor Léwis is generally regarded as a native of Llŷn, for his family moved to Nefyn when he was three years old so that his father could take up his appointment as chief clerk at the Midland Bank in the town. The family home was Uwch y Don, the fourth house beyond the school.

He was educated at Ysgol Nefyn, Pwllheli County School and the University College of Wales Aberystwyth, where he studied law. For many years he was a solicitor with a practice in Pwllheli. He was one of the first solicitors in Wales to be appointed to the judicial bench (previously it was only open to barristers) where he served for eight years as Deputy Circuit Judge in the Crown Court. After taking early retirement as a solicitor, he became a barrister, being called to the Bar at Gray's Inn, London. As a lawyer he fought for the Welsh language to be afforded recognised status in Welsh courts of law, which has largely come about.

From an early age he took a keen interest in politics, standing as a parliamentary candidate at two general elections. As a young man in 1955 he stood for Labour in the Denbigh constituency. At the 1970 General Election he contested the Arfon seat – which includes Nefyn – on behalf of Plaid Cymru, and in a four-cornered fight he came second to Labour, reducing their majority from 12,000 to 2,000.

Dr Léwis has been a prolific author with more than 21 titles to his credit, and he has written books in both Welsh and English. The list includes *Esgid yn Gwasgu* which won the gold Literary Medal at the 1980 National Eisteddfod, and *Geiriaduraeth y Gyfraith: Saesneg-Cymraeg* (an English-Welsh legal dictionary in two large volumes which he calls his *magnum opus*), a work for which he was awarded his PhD and which is accepted as the definitive work by the Courts, Universities and Law Schools in Wales. His autobiography, entitled *Bwystfilod Rheibus* (*Ferocious Beasts*), was included in the list of ten books which were considered for Welsh Book of the Year 2009.

Throughout his life he has been a passionate supporter of the National Eisteddfod of Wales, and from 2002 to 2005 he had the honour of serving as Archdruid of Wales. His bardic name is Robyn Llŷn. He is the first prose writer – as opposed to his predecessors who were all poets – to hold the post, and also the first to be directly elected by all members of the Gorsedd of Bards. The Archdruid is held to be the ceremonial head of the Welsh literary establishment.

Locally he has served the Llŷn community in a number of capacities including Secretary to the Nefyn Agricultural Show, President of Cyfeillion Llŷn (The Friends of Llŷn), and one of the volunteer-writers who keep the local Welsh-language newspaper, *Llanw Llŷn*, going. For many years he and his wife Gwenan, have lived in Rhodfa'r Môr, Nefyn.

Dr Léwis is not only well-known locally in Llŷn but, as a prolific writer, as a former Archdruid of Wales and as an ardent defender of all things Welsh, he is also a figure of national importance.

O Ddrws i Ddrws 2003

In 2003 a new charity, 'O Ddrws i Ddrws' (*from door to door*), was established in Nefyn, and it was officially opened by Prince Charles. 'O Ddrws i Ddrws' is a community transport facility for those folk in Llŷn who find difficulty in getting about because of old age, illness or disability. Such a facility is particularly important in a rural area where public transport is not always readily available. The charity possesses a purpose-built vehicle together with one paid driver, although the scheme depends heavily upon a large number of volunteer drivers who use their own cars to transport people around the peninsula. Users of 'O Ddrws i Ddrws' are asked to make a contribution to the cost of their journeys, for the subsidised scheme is constantly in need of additional funds.

Subsequently the charity acquired a permanent base in the old 'Mace Shop' at the top of Stryd y Plas. Here 'O Ddrws i Ddrws' has an office, while other rooms are used for courses and meetings. This centre, called 'Drws Agored' (the open door), was officially opened by Hywel Williams MP on Friday 4th February 2005. The building also houses several computers which are available for use, and it also hosts Welsh language lessons, art and craft courses and IT classes, all of which are run by Coleg Meirion Dwyfor. A community website called 'Stwdio Nefyn' is also based at the centre.

The Most Photographed Place in Llŷn

Porth Dinllaen is rightly regarded as one of the jewels of Llŷn, for this picturesque 18th century fishing and ship-building village on the beach has been photographed endlessly. In 1994 it was purchased by the National Trust, thus ensuring that it will be protected from future human development and exploitation. In 2004 its attractive setting – the bay with its clustered cottages and the Tŷ Coch Inn – was selected by Craig Rosenberg as one of the locations for his film 'Half Light' which starred the Hollywood actress, Demi Moore.

However, although the protection of the hamlet from human

development is guaranteed, it is predicted that, as the climatic conditions change and as the sea level rises, it will probably be impossible to save Porth Dinllaen and several other National Trust coastal beauty spots. Experts have estimated that sea levels rose by just 2cm during the 18th century, 6cm in the 19th century and 19cm in the 20th century, and it is anticipated that the rise will be far greater during the present century. A National Trust coast and marine adviser has written, 'Over the next 100 years the shape of our coastline will change, and our favourite seaside destinations may not look like they were in our holiday snapshots . . . We need to realise that our environment is not fixed, and that change is inevitable. Society will need to learn to adapt.'[14]

The National Trust has emphasised in its literature that several famous beauty spots, including Porth Dinllaen will almost certainly come under threat from the sea. It will be necessary for such sites 'to evolve naturally – shaped by the power of the sea', warns the National Trust.

A New Primary Health Care Centre for Nefyn 2007
In October 2007 a new Primary Health Care Centre opened in Nefyn to replace the former doctors' premises. This new building was part of the Welsh Assembly Government's ongoing programme of providing improved and integrated health care facilities in larger surgeries across Wales. Nefyn was identified as one of the communities most in need of a new health care centre, and it was the first project of the programme to be completed in North Wales.

The design of the building, which is pleasant, light and airy, embodies 21st century technology, and has been planned to be eco-friendly. It is a timber-framed building with the timber sourced from renewable resources; it includes a heating and hot water system sourced from heat occurring naturally in the ground; and it contains large areas of double glazing to provide maximum natural light and heat retention. The total cost of the project was £1.1 million.

A New Inn Sign for the Bryncynan Inn 2007
'Y Bryncynan' (*the hill of Cynan*) is an ancient hostelry which was certainly in existence in the early 18th century, when the famous blind harpist and composer, John Parry, was reputed to have been born there.

In April 2007 the inn was provided with a new exterior sign, depicting Cynan (Albert Evans Jones) as Archdruid of Wales. He is dressed in his Archdruid's robes, and in his hand he is holding a manuscript copy of his poem 'Mab y Bwthyn' (*son of the cottage*) which tells of a young Welshman's experiences during the Great War. This was the poem for which he won the crown at the Caernarfon National Eisteddfod in 1921 and, appearing so soon after the end of the war, it became extremely popular in Wales.

Albert Evans Jones chose 'Cynan' as his bardic name after Gruffudd ap Cynan, the Welsh Prince, who regained the Kingdom of Gwynedd from the Normans in the late 12th century. Gruffudd ap Cynan, who sometimes landed at Porth Nefyn whilst travelling between Ireland and Gwynedd, was an important patron of the Welsh arts and music. He is generally recognised as the person who laid down rules which afforded structure to the art of the Welsh bards, and therefore it was very appropriate that Albert Evans Jones should have chosen Cynan as his bardic name.

'Cynan' was a Llŷn man, born in Stryd Penlan, Pwllheli. He received his education at Pwllheli County School and the University College of Wales Bangor, and after war service in the Royal Army Medical Corps and later as a chaplain, he attended Bala Calvinistic Methodist Theological College before becoming the minister of a church in Penmaenmawr. In 1931 he joined the staff the Extramural Department of the University College of Wales Bangor, and was Staff Tutor in that department until his retirement in 1960.

Cynan is best remembered as one of the country's leading National Eisteddfod figures and prize winners. Appointed 'Recorder of the Gorsedd of the Bards' in 1934 he was a great reforming Recorder, playing a leading rôle in establishing both the Court and the Council. Furthermore, realising that the ceremonial aspects of the Eisteddfod could be made much more impressive, he set about the task of introducing both drama and dignity into the Gorsedd ceremonies. Two years later he became joint secretary of the National Eisteddfod Council, and in 1967 he was appointed President of the Court. He also adjudicated at the National Eisteddfod. Cynan has the distinction of being the only person to have been elected to the position of Archdruid on two separate occasions – 1950-54 and 1963-66.

As a National Eisteddfod competitor he won the crown three times (Caernarfon 1921, Mold 1923 and Bangor 1931) and the chair once (Pontypool 1924). He was also a playwright, for he won the prize offered for a full length play at the 1931 National, and was commissioned to write another play for the 1957 Eisteddfod. He was also well known for his drama festivals and pageants, such as his historical pageants at Conwy Castle in 1927 and at Caernarfon Castle in 1929 and 1930.

He was a prodigious writer, and it is widely recognised that Welsh literature owes a great deal to Cynan. He published several volumes of poetry, many of which reflect his attitude towards the Great War and his personal experiences of it. Others were inspired by his love of the Llŷn countryside. He translated and adapted the works of other authors; he lectured to extra-mural classes; he directed plays and drama festivals; and he was tutor for a young actors' course arranged by Cwmni Theatr Cymru. His contribution to Welsh literature was recognised by the award of an honorary Doctor of Literature by the University of Wales in 1961, by the award of a CBE in 1949 and by a knighthood in 1969. Cynan died in January 1970.

There has been a long tradition of naming inns and hotels after important personalities, and it is particularly appropriate that the memory of this talented son of Llŷn should have been honoured in the form of a new sign at the Bryncynan Inn.

The Sea Claims a Nefyn Fisherman 2008
One day in April 2008 a Nefyn fisherman went out alone in his boat to fish for whelks, as he normally did. The weather was reasonable and there was no indication that anything untoward was going to happen. Maldwyn Jones of Lôn Cae Rhyg, Nefyn, who had only been fishing full time for about two years, was a non-swimmer, although he was known to be a competent and safe fisherman. Born in Aberdaron, he had lived and worked in England for many years, but had moved back to Llŷn three years previously to take up fishing like certain other members of his family.

On that April day his nephew, Rodney, was also fishing off the northern coast of Llŷn, but he lost sight of his Uncle Maldwyn's boat. When Rodney tried to contact him by radio there was no response, so he turned his boat around and went to investigate. Eventually he could see that his uncle's vessel was heading in a north-easterly direction away from Nefyn. By the time he managed to reach the boat it was going round and round in circles, and it was obvious that there was nobody on board.

A massive sea and air search was launched, involving coastguards, lifeboat crews, police divers and a helicopter from RAF Valley, but there was no trace of the missing fisherman. This search was particularly difficult for the local lifeboat and coastguard personnel, for many of them knew Maldwyn extremely well since the fishing community in Nefyn is so small.

About a month later Maldwyn's body was spotted in the sea by a man from the Wirral, as he was fishing off Trevor. At the inquest into Maldwyn's death the coroner recorded a verdict of 'Accidental Death', noting that the most likely explanation was that he had lost his balance in choppy seas whilst moving about on the deck of his boat and had fallen overboard. The loss of Maldwyn Jones was not only a tremendous tragedy for the members of his family, but it was also very keenly felt by the entire closely-knit community within the town.

A Special Area
The special nature of the area around Nefyn, and indeed the whole of Llŷn, has been recognised by various agencies since the end of the Second World War.

In 1956 large tracts of the peninsula, including the coastline at Porth Dinllaen, were designated Areas of Outstanding Natural Beauty (AONBs).

In 1974 the entire coastline of Llŷn from Aberdesach in the north to Abersoch in the south was awarded the special status of National Heritage Coastline.

In 1998 Cors Geirch and Cors Edern, the marshy areas of land which extend from Rhydyclafdy to Edern, were recognised as prime examples of wetlands and they were officially designated as Sites of Special Scientific Interest (SSSIs).

In 2001 the area known as Pen Llŷn a'r Sarnau (a coastal area which includes the northern coast of the Llŷn Peninsula from Porth Dinllaen southwards, its southern coast and the coast of Cardigan Bay to a point south of the Dyfi Estuary) was identified as a European Marine Special Area of Conservation.

In 2005 North Llŷn Seasearch, a volunteer underwater survey project for marine conservation, investigated the seas around Nefyn and Porth Dinllaen, where they identified a variety of plant and animal species including the important seagrass beds. Seagrass provides an ideal habitat for several species of marine creature.

All this confirms that the Llŷn Peninsula is one of the most important natural environments in Wales, and indeed one of the special marine habitats in the whole of the British Isles.

A New Community Centre for Nefyn 2010
As mentioned in the first chapter, a new community centre, Canolfan Nefyn, was completed at the end of December 2010. This new building is a light and airy, eco-friendly structure with electricity generated from solar panels and the toilets flushed using stored rainwater. The £700,000 needed to erect this building was raised via fund-raising events, donations and grants from various bodies including the Nefyn Town Trust. The centre is now open for a variety of community activities, and it is proving to be an excellent new facility for local people of all ages.

International Fame for Nefyn Girl, Duffy
The Nefyn-born singer-songwriter, Duffy, first burst onto the popular music scene in 2007, and subsequently she has achieved enormous success and

popularity, not only in Wales but right across the world.

Born in 1984, Aimee Ann Duffy grew up in Nefyn with her parents and her two sisters. As a monoglot Welsh speaker she attended Ysgol Nefyn, but when she was ten years old her parents separated, and she went to live with her mother in Pembrokeshire where she had to learn to speak English very quickly. Her mother subsequently remarried, but some time later the family was moved into a 'safe' house on the instructions of the police. It was widely reported in the press at the time that the former wife of Duffy's step father had hired a hitman to kill him.

At the age of 15, having completed her GCSEs, Duffy returned to Nefyn to live with her father. She studied for her 'A' levels at Coleg Meirion Dwyfor, and when she was 19 she entered the S4C television talent show 'Wawffactor' in which she was voted runner up. Whilst studying at Chester University she sang in local clubs in her spare time, for her burning ambition was to become a singer. During her second year at Chester, she abandoned her university studies and returned to Nefyn. For a time she served in a Pwllheli clothing shop and also worked as a barmaid and a waitress.

Her big break came when she was introduced to the founders of Rough Trade Records, who subsequently became her managers. They persuaded her to move to London where they introduced her to other musicians including Bernard Butler (former guitarist with the group 'Suede') with whom she produced the single 'Rockferry'. This was followed by her second single 'Mercy' which reached Number 1 in the charts, and her album 'Rockferry', which became the best selling album of 2008 (with millions of copies sold worldwide) and which reached Number 1 in eleven countries. She has since moved on from Rough Trade Records to be with a new manager and a new musical collaborator.

Since bursting onto the popular music scene, Duffy has been nominated for a string of national and international awards. She won the 'Song of the Year' award for 'Mercy' at the 2008 Mojo Awards; Best Breakthrough Act at the 2008 Q Magazine Awards; an award for her album 'Rockferry' in 2009 at the prestigious US Grammy Awards; Best British Female Solo Act, Best British Breakthrough Act and Best British Album for 'Rockferry' at the 2009 Brit Awards; and 'Mercy' won an award at the 2009 Novello Awards.

On many occasions she has performed on television. She has played at music festivals across Britain, including Glastonbury, the V Festival and Wakestock, as well as major festivals throughout Europe, North America and Australia. She has undertaken tours all over the world including UK and Ireland; Canada and the United States; China, Hong Kong, Singapore and Japan; Australia and New Zealand. She has performed in Russia, Romania and at the Sydney Opera House. Consequently, it is not surprising that she has a following of fans worldwide. She has also taken a small part in a Welsh-language film entitled 'Patagonia'. Since her rise to international prominence Duffy has had numerous features and articles written about her in magazines and newspapers published throughout the world.

It is no exaggeration to say that the people of Nefyn are thrilled with the success that Duffy has achieved in such a short time, and they are extremely proud of this local girl who has risen to global stardom in the world of popular music.

Notes
1. *C&DH* 13/04/1945
2. 'Tŵr Gwylio Nefyn' Robyn Léwis 2010
   '... I ben 'Tŵr', Robyn Léwis, *Llanw Llŷn*, Feb 2012
3. 7th March 1956 – Post Office Archives, London
4. *C&DH* 18/07/1952
5. From an obituary posted on Alumni Bangor website
6. *Daily Telegraph* 15/12/2009
7. *C&DH* 03/08/1979
8. *C&DH* 27/08/1979
9. *C&DH* 21/12/1979
10. *C&DH* 20/07/1984
11. Incident recorded in the British Geological Survey archives
12. *C&DH* 25/4/2002
13. *Cambrian News* 25/4/2002
14. Article on the *Telegraph* website dated 10/11/2008

Bibliography and Sources

Books
Bond, Roland, *Nefyn: The Story of an Ancient Gwynedd Town and Parish*, Gwasg Carreg Gwalch 2008
Davies, Janet, *The Welsh Language: A Pocket Guide*, University of Wales Press/Western Mail 1999
Davies, John Ifor, *Growing Up Among Sailors*, Gwynedd Archives 1983
Dodd, A. H., *A Short History of Wales*, Batsford 2nd impression 1972
Eames, Aled, *Ventures in Sail*, Gwynedd Archives Service, Merseyside Maritime Museum & National Maritime Museum 1987
Elis-Williams, M., *Packet to Ireland*, Gwynedd Archives Service 1984
Evans, Gwynfor, *The Fight for Welsh Freedom*, Y Lolfa 2000
Fenton, R.S., *Cambrian Coasters*, The World Ship Society 1989
Gardner, Juliet, *The Children's War*, Portrait/Imperial War Museum 2005
Gibson, A. D. & Humpage, A. J., *The Geology and Cliff Stability at Nefyn, North Wales – Final Report*, British Geological Survey 2001
Gruffydd, E., *Llŷn*, Gwasg Carreg Gwalch 2003
Illustrated Guide Book: Aberystwyth & North Wales (Southern Edition) Ward Lock 1922-3
Jenkins, Dafydd, *Tân yn Llŷn*, Plaid Cymru Caerdydd 1937, reprinted 1975
Jones, Ivor Wynne, *Shipwrecks of North Wales*, Landmark Publishing 4th edition 2001
Jones, Jennie, *Tomos the Islandman*, Gwasg Carreg Gwalch New edition 1999
Jones, R. Gerallt, *A Place in the Mind: A Boyhood in Llŷn*, Gomer 2004
Jones, Reg Chambers, *Angelsey and Gwynedd: the War Years 1939-45*, Bridge Books, 2008
Lêwis, Robyn, *Bwystfilod Rheibus, Hunangofiant Robyn Lêwis*, Gwasg y Bwthyn 2008
Lêwis, Robyn, 'Tŵr Gwylio Nefyn', an article written for the programme of the Nefyn Carnival 2010
Morgan, Gerald, *A Brief History of Wales*, Y Lolfa 2008
Morgan, Prys & Thomas, David, *Wales: The Shaping of a Nation*, David & Charles, 1984
Morris, Jan, *Wales*, Penguin Books 2000
Morris, Jeff, *The History of the Porthdinllaen Lifeboats* Coventry 1992
Morris, Tom, *Morfa Nefyn*, Gwasg Carreg Gwalch
Morris, Tom, *Morfa Nefyn a Phorthdinllaen*, Gwasg Carreg Gwalch
Parry, Henry, *Wreck and Rescue on the Coast of Wales* D. Bradford Barton Ltd
Pratt, Derrick and Grant, Mike, *Wings across the Border Vol 3*, Bridge Books 2005
Ross, David, *Wales: The History of a Nation*, Geddes & Grosset 2008
Senior, Michael, *Figures in a Landscape Part 2*, Gwasg Carreg Gwalch 2000
Sloan, Roy, *Early Aviation in North Wales*, Gwasg Carreg Gwalch, 2nd edition 2008
Stevens, Catrin, *Telling the Story of Welsh*, Gomer Press 2009
Wallis, Jill, *A Welcome to the hillsides. The Merseyside and North Wales*

experience of evacuation 1939-45, Avid Publications 2000
Wilkinson, Susan, *Mimosa: the life and times of the ship that sailed to Patagonia*, Y Lolfa, 2007
Wilkinson, Susan, *Mimosa's Voyages: Official Logs, Crew List and Masters*, Y Lolfa, 2007
Soldiers Who Died in the Great War Part 28: The Royal Welch Fusiliers, J. B. Hayward & Son, 1988

Newspapers
The Independent 28/10/1998 Obituary : Lord Newborough
The Independent 13/01/1999 Obituary: R. Gerallt Jones
The Straits Times 05/11/1931 Obituary: The Revd A. W. Gough
Caernarfon & Denbigh Herald newspapers – 1893, 1899, 1914, 1916, 1917, 1918, 1922, 1924, 1925, 1940, 1941, 1942, 1943, 1944, 1945, 1948, 1950, 1952, 1979, 1984, 2001, 2002, 2003, 2011
North Wales Chronicle newspapers – 1892, 1906, 1914, 1916, 1917, 1918, 1933, 1936, 1940, 1950, 1973, 1979
Cambrian News 25/4/2002 'Graffiti-daubing in Nefyn'
Daily Telegraph 15/12/2009 Multiple Sclerosis & Stem Cell Treatment.
Daily Telegraph Magazine 02/10/2010 Feature article about Duffy
Daily Mail 03/01/2001 'The Nefyn Landslide'
Daily Post 09/12/2004 'Welsh cottage burners' of 1979
Daily Post 30/04/2008 'Search for a missing Nefyn fisherman'

Other Printed Matter & Manuscript Sources
'Sea in their Blood (an account of the wreck of the *SS Cyprian*)' by Ivor E. Davies published in *Country Quest*, January 1975
The Board of Trade Wreck Report for the Cyprian, Liverpool November 1881
The 1950 Llŷn Pilgrimage to Bardsey – a souvenir booklet
The Census returns for Nefyn 1881, 1891, 1901 & 1911
Nefyn New Cemetery Memorial Inscriptions
Saint Mary's Churchyard Memorial Inscriptions, Nefyn
Sant Mair Churchyard Memorial Inscriptions, Morfa Nefyn
Saint Edern's Churchyard Memorial Inscriptions, Edern
Inscriptions on the Nefyn and Morfa Nefyn War Memorials
Inscriptions on the North Wales Memorial Arch, Bangor
Various Rate Books for Nefyn GAS XB13
Various Electoral Rolls for Nefyn, Gwynedd Archives Service
A Detailed Description of Five Scrap Album Diaries compiled by Fitzherbert Charles Gerald Gough of Gorse Cliff Nefyn, from c1923 – post WW2
Two pedigrees relating to the family of Prebendary A. W. Gough, one providing details his father's pedigree and the other detailing his mother's side of the family
The Board of Trade Wreck Report for the Cyprian 1881
'Labour's Victory in Caernarfonshire: the General Election of 1945', *TCHS* Vol. 63 2002

'Caernarfonshire and its Libraries' by T. Elwyn Griffiths in *TCHS* Vol.33 1972
'Lloyd George and the By-election in the Caernarfon Boroughs 1890' by Emyr Price in *TCHS* Vol. 36 1975
'Lloyd George, Carnarfon Boroughs and Manchester East' by J. Graham Jones in *TCHS* Vol.59 1998
'The Welsh Apprentice of the San Demetrio' by J. Lewis Jones in *Cymru a'r Môr (Maritime Wales)* Vol. 2 1977
Caernarvonshire & Anglesey Postal Directory 1886
Sutton's North Wales Directory 1889-90
Bennett's Directory 1899
Wales Trade Directory 1917
Wales Trade Directory 1928
Wales Trade Directory 1930
Wales Trade Directory 1933
Bennett's Business Directory 1936
Wales Trade Directory 1942
Inland Revenue Valuation Book 1910
Documents relating to the Second World War in Caernarfonshire, GAS XM/1301
Correspondence re Urdd Gobaith Cymru at Porth Dinllaen Farm, GAS XD/32/648 652)
A series of photographs of Prime Minister Clement Attlee with his dog and his cook at his Nefyn holiday accommodation, dated January 1st 1947, NLW
Photograph of Clement Attlee with his wife and two daughters on Nefyn beach dated 1938 (published by the *Guardian* newspaper 29 07 2008)
Catalogue re the sale of Caeau Capel, by John Pritchard & Co 1913, NLW
Leaflet re Urdd camps at Llangranog & Porth Dinllaen 1938, NLW
Extension of railway to Nefyn and Abersoch, GAS XD28/3310
Papers re extension of GWR line to Nefyn 1924, GAS XD2/13200
Ysgol Morfa: Morfa Mlwyddiant 1908-2008
Collection of Wartime Shipping Papers, GAS XM/2002/193
Chronicle of Events in Llŷn, GAS XM/804/38
Photographs of the Nefyn football team 1904 (GAS X/CHS/1274/11/13), 1909 (GAS X/CHS/1274/11/11) and 1926 (GAS X/CHS/1274/11/121)

Maps
OS Map of Nefyn specially enlarged for Land Valuation (Inland Revenue) from the Revision of 1899 and partially revised in 1911
OS Map of Nefyn 25 inches to 1 mile 1918
Plans and Maps re extension of GWR line to Nefyn 1924, GAS XD2A/1665

Internet Sites
Mynegai Morwyr Cymru – Welsh Mariners' Index
The Commonwealth War Graves Commission website
The Porth Dinllaen Lifeboat website
The Porth Dinllaen Coastguard website
The National Coastwatch website

Duffy's official website
Clwb Nefyn United (Nefyn United's website)
Cinema Treasures website – Madryn Hall, Nefyn
Nefyn Golf Club website
Nefyn Sailing Club website
National Library of Wales: Welsh Biography Online
Rhiw.com
The Royal Navy Museum website – 'The Loss of *HMS Hampshire*'
History of Atlantic & Submarine Telegraphy website – Anglo-Irish cables
Urdd Gobaith Cymru website
Marine Conservation Society website – 'North Llŷn Seasearch 2005'
Radar Recollections website – A Bournemouth University project
BBC website – 'WW2 People's War'
Môn Information website – 'The Sinking of *RMS Leinster*'
Nefyn Home website – Reminiscences by Dr Brian Owen, who grew up in Nefyn
News Archive 2003 'King's College London celebrates 50 Years of DNA'
University of Warwick, 'From DNA Structure to Stem Cells'
Telegraph website – 'The fatal landslide at Nefyn' 03/01/2001
Telegraph website – 'Coastal beauty spots to be given up to the sea' 10/11/2008
Glaniad: 'The establishment of the Welsh Settlement in Patagonia'
Western Mail – 'Welsh Back in Fashion in Patagonia' by Steffan Rhys
Times Online – 'Duffy the voice: a star is born' dated 12/01/2008
Alumni Bangor, Bangor University – Obituary of Herbert Rees Wilson
Bangor Civic Society – Names of those killed in the Great War and recorded on the Bangor Memorial Arch

On-line Shop

Our whole catalogue of titles are available on our website

- Walking and Mountaineering
- Regions of Wales / Local Guides
- Maritime Wales
- Welsh Heritage and Culture
- Art and Photography
- Welsh History and Myths
- Children's Books
- ✷ BARGAINS ✷

www.carreg-gwalch.com

Further enjoyable reading on Llŷn

Visit our website for further information:
www.carreg-gwalch.com

Orders can be placed on our
On-line Shop

Further enjoyable reading on History and Heritage

Visit our website for further information:
www.carreg-gwalch.com

Orders can be placed on our
On-line Shop

Further enjoyable reading on Wales and the Sea

Visit our website for further information:
www.carreg-gwalch.com

Orders can be placed on our
On-line Shop

Heritage

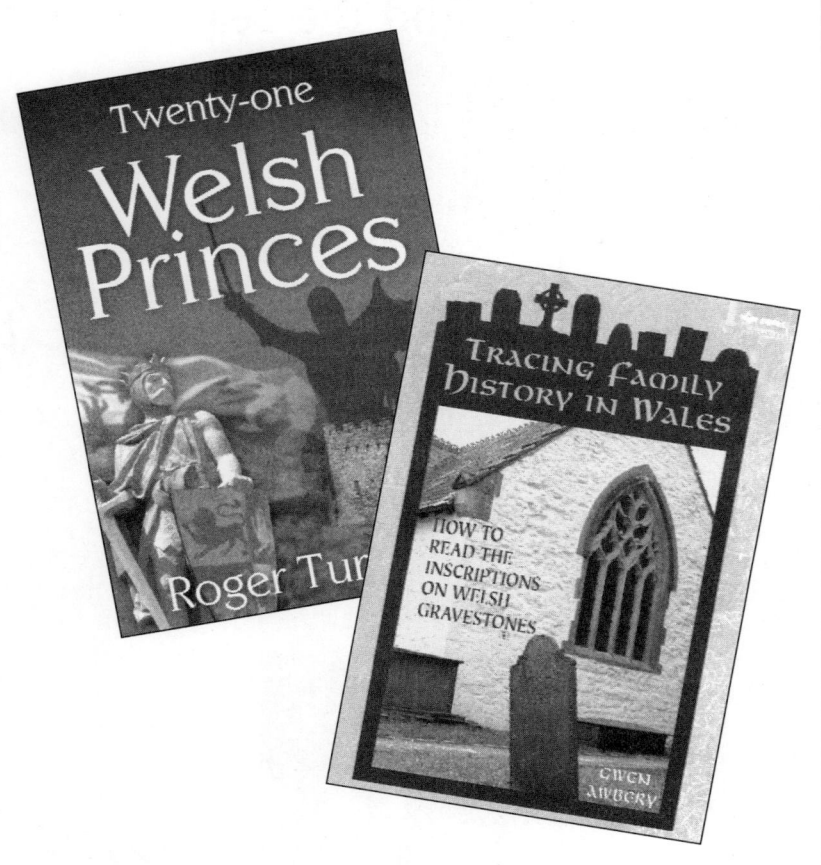

Visit our website for further information:
www.carreg-gwalch.com

Orders can be placed on our
On-line Shop